John Hanson Beadle

The Women's War on Whisky

History, Theory, and Prospects

John Hanson Beadle

The Women's War on Whisky
History, Theory, and Prospects

ISBN/EAN: 9783743325579

Manufactured in Europe, USA, Canada, Australia, Japa

Cover: Foto ©ninafisch / pixelio.de

Manufactured and distributed by brebook publishing software (www.brebook.com)

John Hanson Beadle

The Women's War on Whisky

THE WOMEN'S WAR ON WHISKY:

Its History, Theory, and Prospects.

EMBRACING

A COMPREHENSIVE ACCOUNT OF THE RISE AND PROGRESS OF THE WOMEN'S TEMPERANCE MOVEMENT, WITH SCENES AND INCIDENTS OF THE CAMPAIGN, AND A STATEMENT OF THE BEST MODE OF ENSURING SUCCESS.

BY J. H. BEADLE,

Author of "LIFE IN UTAH," "THE UNDEVELOPED WEST," Etc.

WITH AN

Introductory Article and Statement of the Conditions of Success.

BY DIO LEWIS.

CINCINNATI:
WILSTACH, BALDWIN & CO., 141 & 143 RACE STREET.
1874.

Entered according to Act of Congress, in the year 1874,

By WILSTACH, BALDWIN & CO.,

In the Office of the Librarian of Congress, at Washington.

PREFACE.

A complete history of the Women's Temperance Movement of 1874 can not be written until the war is over, and its phenomena considered and fully understood in the light of its results. The time when this can be done is yet in the future; for it remains to be seen whether the work is not of many months, or even years, in duration. The object of this book is to fill a popular demand for a concise record of the origin and early history of this great Temperance Revival, and of its progress up to the date of publication, when the war is at its height. Another purpose is, by an account of the methods which have been crowned with success, to present to all who wish to try the Ohio plan a manual for guidance—not to propose a substitute for the religious spirit which it seems must, in all cases, be the motive power, but to supply information derived from observation and experience as to the practical working of the movement. As a rule the greatest success has been achieved where there has been systematic organization and labor, accompanied by devout religious exercises and a constant looking to God for his blessing and guidance in every step of the work.

INTRODUCTION:

BY DIO LEWIS.

There was trouble at our house when I was a small boy. My father had forgotten everything but drink. There were five of us small people. Our mother, with her own hands, provided for all. She earned and cooked our food, cut and made our clothes; in brief, was father, mother, general provider, cook, housekeeper, and nurse. In addition to all this she was the victim of abuse and violence. Often she would cry in the presence of her children, and sometimes, when she could bear it no longer, she would drag her weary limbs up into the garret. We knew what she went up there for, and listened. Sometimes we could hear her say, "Oh God, help me! help me! help me? Oh Lord, how long, how long!" Then she would keep very still for awhile. When she came down to us again her cheeks were wet, but her face shone like an angel's. She taught us to pray. We grew up with a very large estimate of the power of prayer. The day was never so dark at our house that mother could not go up into the garret and open the clouds.

To-day, more than forty years after those darkest times, I believe in my heart that woman's prayer is the most powerful agency on earth.

Nineteen years ago, when I first began to speak in

public, I prepared a lecture upon the Potency of the Prayers of Women in Grog Shops, which, during these years, I have delivered more than three hundred times. In about twenty towns the plan has been tried. Among the largest of these towns I may mention Dixon, Illinois, and Battle Creek, Michigan, where fourteen years ago the work was attempted, and Manchester, New Hampshire, where the "Woman's Temperance Movement" was inaugurated five years ago. In each of these places I presented the scheme precisely as in Southern Ohio, and know of no reason why the grand march did not begin before the last week of the year 1873. All we know is that God was not ready to move on the hearts of His people.

Lecturing before the lyceums of Ohio during last December, I gave two evenings to the discussion of Women's Prayer Meetings in Saloons. In Hillsboro and Washington C. H., where this lecture was given, the women rose at once and declared they were ready. I saw that the hour had struck. The world knows the story.

I have not a doubt that the women of America will rid the country of dram-shops if they can preserve the Christ-spirit in which they have begun, continue their combined movements against the enemy, give the politicians and *wise* men a wide berth, and keep themselves in the spirit of humble prayer before God.

DIO LEWIS,
Boston, Mass., *March* 5, 1874.

CHAPTER I.

ORIGIN OF THE MOVEMENT.

THE Women's War on Whisky, now in progress in Ohio and some other States, is unparalleled among the phenomena of the age. When we consider the apparent feebleness of the agencies employed, as contrasted with the mighty forces previously brought to bear in the same direction, their comparative results, we must credit this movement with the highest character of success—that which consists in educing great results from limited means. Other movements have been heralded by immense and ingenious preparation, and nursed into life, as it were, slowly and painfully; but this, as if without concert or previous calculation, seemed to spring at once into full life and astonishing vigor—like Minerva, full-orbed and armor-clad, from the brain of Jupiter.

And yet it was not a causeless, aimless excitement. On a completer view, all the movements hitherto for the suppression of intemperance seem but as preparatory to some such movement as this—a mighty moral and social revolution accomplishing that which the law could not. Before entering upon a detailed history of the movement, a brief review of the causes leading to it is in order.

The intemperate use of intoxicating liquors has been in all ages justly regarded as a great scourge of humanity; and this alike in the lower and higher stages of civilization. The refining influences which moderated all other appetites and assuaged all other evils seemed almost ineffective as to this. In vain the moralist, satirist, priest, and law-giver, of every age, persuaded, ridiculed, and shamed its voluntary victims; in vain they thundered against its agents with the terrors of human or divine vengeance; the same madness seized on successive devotees, and the same stream of death rolled on. Ancient and modern literature alike abound in myths and emblems symbolizing the terrors of the alcoholic curse. It is fabled as the cup of Circe, transforming men to swine; or the devil which entered men's mouths to steal away their brains. Now it is represented as with venom which biteth like a serpent and stingeth like an adder; again, as the deadly upas tree, in whose shade myriads, in spite of warning, sunk to sleep only to wake in death; and again, as the serpent of the still, whose fiery bite sends poison through the body, racking every nerve and joint with horrors of which language affords no adequate description. And when moralist, satirist, and philosopher had spoken, the inspired Messenger added the dread sentence: "No drunkards shall inherit the kingdom of God."

Yet, in spite of warnings, threats, and the terrible evidences daily before their eyes, multitudes pressed on; and, after two thousand years of moralizing, the evil was attacked by legislators. And with what result? Those who have studied the case most carefully seem divided between three opinions: One class maintains that prohibitory legislation has done great harm and no good whatever; another, that it has done a little good and no harm; and a third, that it has done neither good nor harm; and the matter remains just where it did. Two hundred years and more after the first enactment of laws for the discouragement of the sale of intoxicating drinks in England, and after a fair trial of prohibition for a quarter of a century in several of the States of the Union, in the year of Grace, 1874, we find in the United States this state of facts: Two hundred thousand rum-holes spread disease and death through all ranks of society. A quarter of a million drunkards, and a million moderate drinkers, from whom the ranks of the former are steadily recruited, attest the power of this appetite. From half a million women a wail of anguish is wafted over an otherwise happy land; and over the graves of forty thousand drunkards, annually, goes up the mourning cry of the widow and orphan, appealing to the justice of Heaven against the injustice of man.

The chief evils of the traffic in ardent spirits have fallen on women; and it was eminently fitting that women should inaugurate the work for its destruction. At one time, and without apparent concert, notes of preparation were heard in various places. Four towns in Ohio claim the honor of having been the first—Washington Court House, Hillsboro, Wilmington, and Springfield. In the last-named place several attempts were made as early as October, 1873, to enforce existing laws against the indiscriminate sale of liquors. At that time Mrs. E. D. Stewart, better known to the friends of temperance and woman suffrage as "Mother Stewart," took up the cause of a poor woman whose husband had long been of the class "habitual drunkard," and assisted her to prosecute certain dealers under the Adair law. She found great difficulty in inducing any lawyer to take the case; but finally Mr. Rawlings did so, with the understanding that "Mother Stewart" was to help the prosecution. She "read up" on the law, hunted out the witnesses, and made a case beyond a reasonable doubt. She then collected a number of ladies to attend the court during the trial, and give "moral support." With the women, the law, and the evidence against him, the dealer lost the case, and judgment was given against him by a jury in the justice's court for $300. "Mother Stewart" examined the witnesses, and made the opening speech, as the law allowed her to do before a justice; but the dealer, backed by the Liquor-sellers' Association, appealed to a higher court, and there she was barred out.

A few Sundays after she made a round of the city, taking note of the various places where the law was violated, and entering a prominent saloon, in partial disguise, bought a glass of liquor and carried it away to exhibit before the next temperance meeting. Those who were present when she held up the glass and told the story of a broken Sabbath and violated law, describe the scene as theatrical and impressive. She then published and circulated, anonymously, an "Appeal to the Women of Springfield," signed "A Drunkard's Wife." This was powerfully written, and created great excitement. A petition was then circulated and signed by a thousand women or more, praying the city council to make use of their power under the 199th section of the Municipal Code, and abate the saloons as nuisances—and here occurred the first defeat. Of the ten councilmen one is a brewer, another a distiller, another indifferent on the subject, and only three pronounced and radical temperance men. The ladies, however, continued earnestly in the work of a legal reform, and had collected materials for fifty indictments against liquor dealers before the inauguration of the regular Women's War. Thus it has resulted that the two contests, that by the Law and that by aid of the Gospel, have gone along simultaneously in Springfield; but whether this conjunction is favorable to success may well be doubted.

ORIGIN OF THE MOVEMENT.

At Hillsboro, Highland county, some action was taken looking toward a temperance campaign, on the 23d of December. Dr. Dio Lewis had lectured there a few days before, and made the same suggestions as at Washington.

At Wilmington it is claimed that a movement very similar to this was inaugurated some fifteen years ago by Mrs. Sarah Smith and Mrs. Mary Hadley, two Quaker ladies of that place. Mary Hadley used to visit and remain at the saloons for days together, There was one fellow she was quite friendly with. She would come in the morning, and say: "Well, friend, how does thee do? I've come to spend the day with thee again." Pretty soon some fellow would come in, and, thinking she was one of the family, would call for his drink quite unconcerned. About the time he was lifting it he would feel a tap on his shoulder, and Mary would say in her sweet voice and pleasant way: "Friend, does thee know thee is taking poison?" Last December the people of Wilmington were organizing for a temperance campaign some days before Dio Lewis came to Washington. But, as regards a regular organization, a plan of campaign and effective work persevered in until crowned with successs, Washington C. H. must be held as justly entitled to the honor of initiating The Women's War on Whisky.

CHAPTER II.

EARLY VICTORIES.

On the evening of December 24, 1873, the Lyceum and Lecture Association of Washington C. H. had, in its regular course, a lecture on "Our Girls," by Dr. Dio Lewis, the celebrated author of a system of gymnastics and of works on "Health," "Hygiene," etc. Incidental to his main subject, the Doctor referred at some length to the use of tobacco and ardent spirits, and the havoc they were working in the social life of America. It is impossible to say anything new on the evils of intemperance; the Doctor did better—he suggested a new plan for fighting the evil, and in so doing inaugurated the grandest movement of the age. He gave an account of a plan the ladies of his native place in New York had adopted for closing the drinking places. There were five in the place (it was a manufacturing town), and numbers of the men who worked in the mills wasted the means of their families' support in tippling. At length a number of young boys were made drunk one Saturday evening at one of these places; then the women rose in despair and cried unto God for help. It entered the minds of some of them to suggest prayer and personal intercession with the saloon keepers, and in their desperation this method was adopted. A band of ladies, the praying mothers of the place, stood up and with clasped hands, forming a circle which just reached around the little church, pledged each other before God never to give over their labors and prayers until the last drinking place in town was closed. They made a little banner, embroidered with a picture of a little girl at a well, giving a drink of water to a boy, and under this simple device they went out day after day to their chosen work. They sang, prayed, and sang again with each saloon-keeper, then presented their request for him to quit the business, and in a few days all the dealers had yielded but one. He plead that it was the only business he had by which to support his family. Then the ladies came forward with a generous proposition: "They would support his family; only quit selling liquor, to the danger of their husbands and sons, and they would cheerfully earn the money with their needles, and between them would support his family!" Deep shame made him silent, and before another day he, too, was pledged to sell no more. Nineteen years have passed and that town is still free from saloons! The Doctor thought the same plan would succeed in Washington, and offered to meet as many as would organize the next day.

Christmas morning, at nine o'clock, a large number of the foremost men and women of the place met at the Methodist church, and then and there was organized the movement against the liquor traffic, which will pass into history as the "Washington Court House Plan." Eighty ladies enlisted at once, and on the 26th of December began the work.

Their plan was to visit the saloons in force, and, after asking permission, hold a regular prayer meeting, asking the blessing of God on the proprietor and his family. After a due season of prayer and song they presented what is now generally known as the "Dealers' Pledge," and requested him to sign it. It simply pledged him never to sell intoxicating liquors again in Washington. If he declined, they renewed their visits; but it was not their policy to hold any arguments. They merely sang and prayed for the Divine influence upon his heart. The number of saloons there when the movement began was ten. There were also four drug stores, selling without particular discrimination; these were requested to, and soon did, sign a pledge to sell only on the prescription of a regular physician.

By the first day of January, 1874, one week from the time of organizing, one-half the liquor dealers had surrendered unconditionally, some shipping their liquor back to the wholesale dealers, and others pouring it into the gutters. For the next three days the campaign was at its height. While the ladies went on their rounds, the men in sympathy with them and a large number of ladies remained in the church in continued prayer meeting; at the close of each prayer the bell was tolled, and the crusaders were cheered on in their work by the knowledge that another supplication had ascended for their success. The band now numbered a hundred and fifty ladies. The saloon-men who remained were the most obstinate of the class, and now began to refuse the ladies admittance; then the latter knelt in front of the door and prayed all the more fervently for God's grace to soften and convert the dealer. One by one the dealers yielded to their persuasions and prayers, and finally, on the fourth day of January, the glad news was telegraphed that not a drop of any thing intoxicating could be purchased for a beverage in Washington. A campaign of song and prayer had, in eleven days, closed ten saloons and pledged four druggists to sell only on prescription.

But the ladies, rightly judging that they had a great deal more to do, commenced laying a broader foundation to make their work permanent. The mass meetings, which had been held every evening, at the churches alternately, were continued, as were the morning prayer meetings; and the personal pledge was industriously circulated. In a short time a thousand signatures were obtained to the personal pledge.

The doctors were also called upon, and generally agreed that they would never prescribe ardent spirits when any substitute could be used, and in no case without a personal examination of the patient.

The property-holders' pledge was next in order, reading as follows:

"We, the undersigned, property-holders of Washington, do hereby pledge ourselves not to lease or rent our property to any person or persons, to be used as saloons, nor to allow any dealings of the liquor traffic to be carried on upon or in any property or premises belonging to us."

This was signed, with only two or three exceptions, by all who owned property that could be used for liquor selling.

For a brief space the ladies rested after their victory; but there was a great deal more to do. This enemy is not one that will retire after one defeat, nor two, nor three. Washington had a "John Allen," a "wickedest man," who was willing to do mischief for mischief's sake. A man named Slater took counsel of his priest and lawyer, who informed him that whisky selling was "a legitimate business under the laws of Ohio," and he would be sustained in it. Accordingly he opened a saloon a little meaner than any of those which had been suppressed. The ladies came in force, with singing, prayer, and eloquent pleadings; but he resisted all, and affected to treat the whole matter with contempt. Only a few of the lowest and most desperate tipplers would visit his house while the ladies occupied it; but he sold liquor right over their heads to what few customers he had. At length there came a fearfully cold day, and Slater built no fire, but sprinkled water on the floor and opened both front and back doors, creating quite a draught, being determined to freeze them out. The ladies "guessed they could stand the cold, if he could stand the cold and whisky too," and heroically stuck to their work. The town marshal was on hand most of the time, warmed boards for them to stand on, and finally built a fire in the street. The next move was to erect a "tabernacle," a portable frame building, with one side open and fitted up with stove and seats. This they set up in front of the saloon, and being divided into relief committees kept up all-day prayer meetings. A rumor then spread about town, causing immense excitement for awhile, that Slater was backed by a Cincinnati firm of liquor dealers, who had pledged $5,000 to break down the movement. On the 15th of January a clear case of violating the Adair law was made out against Mr. Slater, and he was compelled to suspend. Then came one Bigsby, evidently a "lewd fellow of the baser sort," who announced himself the agent of a Cincinnati firm, and proposed to establish a wholesale liquor store in Washington. The ladies sought him, but he laughed at their prayers, ridiculed their pleadings, and generally proved himself a man sold wholly to Satan. One lady insisted on knowing the name of his Cincinnati firm, proposing to correspond with them, to which he replied that he could not allow her to enter upon a correspondence with liquor dealers unless she could show the "written consent of her husband under the Adair law." But he proved to be a romancer, and, as no Cincinnati firm has been found to acknowledge him, it is evident that he added the sin of lying to that of resisting the gospel of temperance.

For a few days the ladies congratulated themselves that their work was done, but with all their experience they had underrated the devices of the enemy. A mile or so south of town was a wayside saloon, kept by one James Sullivan, and just out of town, on the Chillicothe pike, a beer hall by Charlie Beck; and these two gave them more trouble than all the ten in the city. There is always a class who "must have liquor," or think so. The vast majority of men who drink habitually or occasionally, but still moderately, will not go far out of their way to get liquor, and to shut up the saloons generally stops their drinking. But the "confirmed" class now centered their patronage on Beck and Sullivan, and there was too much money in the business for them to give it up readily. But nothing daunted, the ladies prepared for a vigorous campaign against the two saloons, though both were outside of the corporation and not included in the original pledge the crusaders had made with each other. About this time the novel method of fighting whisky with prayer and song began to attract the attention of the press and people elsewhere, and the writer concluded to spend "a few days" in taking notes of the matter. The "few days" have stretched to seven weeks, and the end is not yet.

I reached Washington at noon of January 20th, and, seeking Mr. Beck's beer garden, found him in a state of terrible nervousness, as the ladies had spent the forenoon in front of his place. He evidently regarded me as a spy, but was much mollified when assured that I was only a journalist, and made voluminous complaint in "High Dutch" and low English:

"I got no vitnesses. Dem vimens dey set up a shob on me. But you don't bin a 'bitual drunkard, eh? No, you don't look like him. Vall, coom in, coom in. Vat you vant, beer or vine? I dells you dem vimins is shust awful. Py shinks, dey build a house right in the shreet, and stay mit a man all day a singin', and oder foolishness. But dey don't git in here once agin, already."

In obedience to his invitation I had entered by the side door—the front was locked and barred—to find four customers indulging in liquor, beer, and pigs' feet. One announced himself as an "original Granger," a second as a retired sailor, while the others were non-committal. They stated that two spies had just applied for admission—"men who would come in and drink, then go and swear they were habitual drunkards under the Adair law"—and that accounted for Mr. Beck's suspicions of me.

The Adair law I find everywhere to be the great horror of saloon-keepers. It allows any wife or child, or other relative directly interested, to prosecute for the sale of liquor to husband or father; and almost any one may prosecute for the sale of liquor to a "habitual drunkard."

Whether such a law be just or constitutional, there is great dispute; but it is evident that it gives great opportunity for fraud and blackmailing. It is, however, just now the strong rock of defense of the Ohio temperance people; and it may be that by its enforcement some saloon-keepers have been driven out of the business who would have withstood the prayers of an archangel and all the tears that sorrowing pity ever shed.

Mr. Beck kept open house nearly all that night; the

sounds of revelry were plainly heard in town, and in the morning several drunken men came into town, one of whom tumbled down in a livery stable, and went to sleep on a manure-pile, from which he was carried to the lock-up. Matters were evidently coming to a crisis, and I went out early; but the ladies reached there in force just before me. I met Mr. Beck hurrying into town to consult his lawyer, or, as he phrased it, "to see mein gounsel venn I no got a right to my own broperty."

The main body of the ladies soon arrived, and took up a position with right center on the door-step, the wings extending each way beyond the corners of the house, and a rearward column along the walk to the gate. In ludicrous contrast the routed revelers, who had been scared out of the saloon, stood in a little knot fifty feet away, still gnawing at the pigs' feet they had held on to in their hurried flight; while I took a convenient seat on the fence. The ladies then sang:

"Oh, do not be discouraged, for Jesus is your friend,
He will give you grace to conquer, and keep you to the end."

As the twenty or more clear, sweet voices mingled in the enlivening chorus—

"I'm glad I'm in this army," etc.—

The effect was inspiring. I felt all the enthusiasm of the occasion, while the pigs'-feet party, if they did not feel guilty, certainly looked so. The singing was followed by a prayer from Mrs. Mills Gardner. She prayed for the blessing of God on the temperance cause generally, and in this place particularly; then for Mr. Beck, his family and friends, his house and all that loved him, and closed with an eloquent plea for guidance in the difficult and delicate task they had undertaken. In one respect the prayer was unsurpassed; it was eminently fitting to the place and occasion. As the concluding sentences were being uttered, Mr. Beck and his "gounsel" arrived. The ladies paid no attention to either, but broke forth in loud strains:

"Must Jesus bear the cross alone?
No, there's a cross for me,"

When the lawyer borrowed some of my paper, whispering at the same time: "I must take down their names. Guess I shall have to prosecute some of them before we stop this thing."

I should need the pen of an Irving and pencil of a Darley to give any adequate idea of the scene. On one side a score of elegant ladies, singing with all the earnestness of impassioned natures; a few yards away, a knot of disturbed revelers, uncertain whether to stand or fly; half-way between, the nervous Beck, bobbing around like a case of fiddle-strings with a hundred pounds of lager-beer fat hung on them, and on the fence by the ladies a cold-blooded lawyer and excited reporter scribbling away as if their lives depended on it. It was painful from its very intensity.

The song ended, the presiding lady called upon Mrs. Wendell, and again arose the voice of prayer—so clear so sweet, so full of pleading tenderness, that it seemed she would, by the strength of womanly love, compel the very heavens to open and send down in answer a spark of divine Grace that would turn the saloon-keeper from his purpose. The sky, which had been overcast all morning, began to clear, the occasional drops of rain ceased to fall, and a gentle south wind made the air soft and balmy. It almost seemed that nature had joined in the prayer.

Again the ladies sung:

> "Are there no foes for me to face,"

With the camp-meeting chorus:

> "O, how I love Jesus,
> Because he first loved me."

As this song concluded, the lawyer suddenly stepped forward and said:

"Now, ladies, I have a word to say before this performance goes any further. Mr. Beck has employed me as his attorney. He can not speak good English, and I speak for him here. He is engaged in a legitimate business, and you are trespassers on his property and right. If this thing is carried any further you will be called to account in the court, and I can assure you the court will sustain the man. He has talked with you all he desires to. He does not want to put you out forcibly; that would be unmanly, and he does not wish to act rudely. But he tells you to go. As his attorney I now warn you to desist from any further annoyance."

Again the ladies sang:

> "My soul be on thy guard,
> Ten thousand foes arise."

And Mrs. Carpenter followed with a fervent prayer for the lawyer and his client; but they had fled the scene, leaving the house locked up. After consultation the ladies decided to leave Mr. Beck's premises and take a position on the adjoining lot. They sent for the "tabernacle," a rude frame building they had used in front of Slater's saloon. This they erected on an adjoining lot, put up immense lights to illuminate the entrance to the beer garden, and kept up a guard from early morning till midnight. Legal proceedings were at once instituted, and two weeks afterward the following dispatch appeared in the Cincinnati papers:

> WASHINGTON C. H., OHIO, February, 4.
> Tell Beadle, of the Commercial, that my *gounsel* has had demperance meeting and tabernacle abated as a nuisance.
> CHAS. BECK.

It was too true. An injunction was granted, and then the temperance party had recourse to the law. One Mrs. Frazier brought suit against Sullivan and Beck, under the Adair law, and the former was soon compelled to suspend. Mr. Beck held out for a short time, then yielded good-humoredly to the ladies, and the place was again clear. Then came one Passmore with six kegs of beer, and opened out in one of the deserted saloons. His first visitors were one hundred women; and they stayed with him all day. At night he yielded, and signed a pledge to never sell liquor again in Washington. It was noted by the transfer agent at Morrow that six kegs of beer were shipped to Washington one morning and ten sent back the next night. Washington Court House remains free from the curse, and such a healthful public sentiment has been created that for years to come it will be almost impossible for a saloonist to get a foothold in the place. All honor to the fair and brave Washingtonians, and may they long enjoy the fruits of their victory.

Wilmington, where the movement next began, the county town of Clinton county, had a shorter campaign, and fully as complete a victory. On Saturday evening, January 3d, all the churches united in a temperance organization; and on the 5th sixty-two ladies entered upon the work, visiting the four drug stores and eleven saloons. In three days more the ladies came in bands from the surrounding country to assist; two hundred women engaged in the work, and on the 14th the last saloon surrendered! In nine days the ladies of Clinton county closed eleven saloons, and obtained pledges from the four druggists.

The movement next spread to the neighboring towns of Sabina and Clarksville. Both were cleared of saloons in a few days. But the movement had now ceased to be local, and was spreading in all directions, half a dozen fresh places being aroused every day. We must now follow its history in general terms, rather than in special detail.

CHAPTER III.

RAPID EXTENSION OF THE WORK.

FRIEND and foe alike have been astonished at the rapid progress of the temperance work. For a few days its opponents sneered, and the public were simply indifferent; but as it spread, grew, and mightily prevailed, there were abundant prophecies as to the result. Some, that it would degenerate soon into a mere burlesque; more, that it would run into a wild fanaticism, disgraceful to religion and hurtful to morals; or that it would create a temporary enthusiasm, to be followed in a few weeks by a reaction and more drinking than before. The best friends of temperance were not without apprehensions that the popular feeling might run into a mere wild crusade, ungoverned by reason and unproductive of good. It is only fair to say that both friend and foe have been disappointed. The movement has gained in steadiness as it increased in power; and instead of fanaticism, we see in places where it has last been inaugurated, a cool precision of judgment and practical arrangement of details almost military in exactness. Nor has the movement encountered that fierce opposition one would naturally have expected. It is a noteworthy fact that Washington and Hillsboro, the starting points, are the only places where a vigorous legal fight was made against the reform; meanwhile scores of other places have been swept clean of saloons. The matter has now passed beyond the domain of the merely sensational, and the conflict of the women of Ohio with the whisky power is a fixed fact, likely to continue in full vigor for months, and to affect the politics and society of many sections, if not of the whole State, for a much longer period. The very genius of primitive Christianity seems to inspire some of these praying women, and their exhortations warm the coldest hearts like a new gospel, second only to the fervid preaching of the Apostolic fishermen of Galilee.

At Hillsboro, in Highland county, the movement was cotemporary with that at Washington, but has encountered many difficulties. By the middle of January a hundred women were at work, and all the better part of the community, in sympathy with them, were holding mass meetings every night, circulating the pledge and giving moral support by every means in their power. One-half the saloons had been closed, and half the druggists had given the usual pledge, when the first serious hindrance to the movement occurred. Dr. W. H. H. Dunn, the leading druggist, at the beginning of the work presented the following:

"CONCESSION OF THE PALACE DRUG STORE TO DIO DEWIS.

"LADIES—In compliance with your request I give you this promise: That I will carry on my business in the future as I have in the past; that is to say, in the sale of intoxicating liquors I will *comply with the law;* nor will I sell to any person whose father, mother, wife, or daughter gives me a written request not to make such sale.

"W. H. H. DUNN."

I visited Hillsboro during the height of the contest, and gave this account of the situation while the ladies were besieging Dr. Dunn:

All this damp winter day, from ten o'clock this morning till now, four in the afternoon, this prayer and praise has continued; and as I drop my pen a moment the air is filled with the melody of the old camp-meeting tune:

> "Jesus sought me when a stranger,
> Wandering from the fold of God."

Passing by the back entrance occasionally into the drug store, I find the doctor and his clerk whiling away their time as best they can; perhaps one-twentieth of their time being taken up in actual business. The doctor does not swear exactly, or abuse the ladies, but sometimes he looks very, very weary. The front door is locked, and the few customers work a devious way around, a boy being on the watch with careful instructions "to admit no suspicious characters." The doctor says his business three weeks ago amounted to sixty dollars a day, while now it is seldom over ten. He dwells bitterly on the facts that he "does a legitimate business, not violating any law of State or city; that he has always been a temperate man, and as long as God gives him strength he will keep his temper, and treat the ladies respectfully, waiting for this fanatical frenzy to wear out."

A fresh detail of women has just arrived, and, after a lengthy prayer, are dealing out old "Coronation" in heart-moving tones. The towns-people go and come their accustomed ways with little notice, but it is curiously comical to notice strangers and country people. They begin to step gingerly about a square off; as they get nearer steadily soften their steps, and finally take off their hats and edge their way slowly around the open-air prayer meeting as one would pass a funeral. It reminds me strongly of sights I have witnessed in Catholic countries, where people do their praying in the open air just like any other business.

The next morning (January 31st) Hillsboro awoke to a sensation. Scattered in all the hall-ways and posted in the most conspicuous places was this placard:

"NOTICE TO THE LADIES OF HILLSBORO."

"WHEREAS, Many of you, among whom are: Mesdames William Scott, William Trimble, Sams, W. O. Collins, J. M. Boyd, A. Evans, Reece Griffith, Jonah Langley, William Hoyt, Carolina Miller, Wash. Doggett, W. P. Bernard, Misses Maria Stewart, Rachel Conrad, Sallie Stevenson, Maggie Bowles, Clara Rhodes, Annie Wilson, Grace Gardner, Jennie Harris, Emma Grand-Girard, Mollie Van Winkle, Emily Grand-Girard, Libby Kirby. Ella Dill, Laura Rockhold, Eddy, Alice Speese, Kate Trimble, Alice Boardman and sister [fifty more names follow], who are aided by the following named gentlemen: Messrs. E. L. Ferris, H. S. Fullerton, Samuel Amen, Asa Haynes, J. J. Brown, J. S. Black, W. C. Barry, E. Carson, Joseph Glasscock, William Scott, Thomas Barry, S. E. Hibben & Son, T. C. Lytle, R. S. Evans, L. McKibben, R. Griffiths, J. L. Boardman, John Cowgill, Lewis Ambrose, H. Scarborough, William Ambrose, Wash. Doggett, H. Swearingen, Rev. E. Grand-Girard, and many others.

"And who, although not directly participating in your daily proceedings, are, nevertheless, counseling and advising you in your unlawful proceedings by subscriptions of money, and encouragement in the commission of daily trespasses upon my property, since the 24th day of December last, by reason of which my legitimate business has been obstructed, my feelings outraged, and my profession and occupation sought to be rendered odious, by reason of which I have suffered great pecuniary damage and injury, Therefore, you and each of you, together with your husbands (or such as may have them), and the persons who are thus aiding you with their money, encouragement and advice in your unlawful proceedings, are hereby notified that I can not, nor will not, longer submit to your daily trespasses on my property and injury to my business.

"While I am willing to excuse your action in the past, I can not submit to such outrages in the future. Cherishing no unkind hostility toward any one, but entertaining the highest regard for the ladies of Hillsboro, distinguished heretofore as they have been for their courtesy, refinement, and Christian virtues, I feel extremely reluctant to have to appeal to the law for protection against their riotous and unlawful acts.

"You are therefore hereby further notified that if such action and trespasses are repeated, I shall apply to the laws of the State for redress and damages for the injuries occasioned by reason of the practices of which I complain.

"All others aiding and encouraging you by means of money or otherwise are also notified that I shall hold them responsible for such advice and encouragement. Yours respectfully,

"W. H. H. DUNN."

An immense mass meeting of the temperance party met at nine o'clock; it was unanimously resolved to go on in the work; in one hour a frame tent was erected in the street in front of Dunn's store, and eighty-three ladies took possession, keeping up an all-day prayer meeting. The same attorney who had been "gounsel" for Mr. Beck at Washington, was sent for to serve Mr. Dunn; and in a day or two Judge Safford, of the Probate Court, issued the following to over two hundred of the temperance party:

"You are hereby notified and warned that David Johnson and W. H. H. Dunn, plaintiffs, have this day obtained an order of temporary injunction and a restraining order in an action pending in the Court of Common Pleas, for the said county of Highland, wherein they are plaintiffs, and you, the above named persons, are defendants, and have given an undertaking according to law. This is, therefore, to command you, the said above named defendants, each and all of you, from using for praying, singing, exhorting, or any other purpose, a certain plank and canvas structure or shanty, erected on High street, in Hillsboro, Ohio, in front of the drug store of said W. H. H. Dunn; and it is further ordered that you, said defendants, are ordered to remove the said structure or

RAPID EXTENSION OF THE WORK. 29

shanty forthwith, and each and every part of the same, whether plank or canvas, and you are each and all hereby restrained and enjoined from re-erecting or replacing the said structure, or any similar structure, in said locality or upon said street, to the annoyance of the said W. H. H. Dunn; and it is further ordered that you, the said defendants, each and all of you, are hereby enjoined and restrained from singing, praying, exhorting, or making a noise and disturbance in front of said drug store of said W. H. H. Dunn, or on the sidewalk, or on the steps thereof, or in the vicinity thereof, to his annoyance, or from trespassing in or upon his said premises, or in any manner interrupting his said business, and this you will in no wise omit under the penalty of the law.

"Witness my hand and the seal of said Court at Hillsboro, this 31st day of January, 1874.

[SEAL] "J. K. PICKERING, Clerk.

" A true copy: C. T. PAPE, Sheriff."

In consequence of this order, in the dead of night the "faithful" submissively—

"Folded their tent like the Arabs,
And silently stole away,"

And at the dawn of day there was naught to mark where the "tabernacle" had stood. It had mysteriously disappeared. The defendants retained the services of M. J. Williams, Esq., of Washington C. H., and Judge Matthews and J. H. Thomson, of Hillsboro; Dunn employed Messrs. Sloan, Buson, Collins, and Parker, and a legal contest of the greatest interest began. The case was argued at length before Judge Steele, of the Circuit Court; the ladies attended in great numbers; the Women's War in all its bearings was discussed by the counsel, and the matter finally decided on a mere technicality. It was held that David Johnson was improperly joined with Mr. Dunn, as the former merely owned the property, not the business; the merits of the case were left untouched, the temporary injunction was dissolved, and the parties left to their remedies at law. The legal aspects of this and similar cases will be found under the proper heading.

Greenfield, in the northern part of the same county, entered upon the temperance war with unusual vigor. The movement began on the 12th of January, and in six weeks eleven saloons were closed, and three druggists had signed the pledge. The pledge of personal abstinence was meanwhile signed by 2,640 persons. But one drug store, kept by a Mr. Clinton, remained open, and notoriously sold more liquor than any three of the saloons. Week after week the persevering women kept up their labors. The affair was conducted with the utmost courtesy on both sides. Mr. Clinton never locked his door against them, nor did they ever display impatience or ill-temper. I can not give a better idea of the spirit of love and piety animating the crusaders than to copy from the Secretary's reports. Every night, in mass meeting, the Secretary of the Ladies' Temperance League read a report of work done during the day, most of them in spirit like these:

"GREENFIELD, O., January 23, 1874.

"At the close of the hour of prayer, held by the business men of our community this morning, the Ladies' League assembled at the church. After commending our cause to the Heavenly Father, as has always been our custom, we started forth.

"It was intended to call on Dr. T. S. McGurrough again this morning; but on reaching the drug store we learned that it had not been opened since his return from Cincinnati, and our first visit was to Mr. Kaiser. We presented our supplications for him to God in songs and prayers, and then commended to him the dealers' pledge. But our hearts were not prepared to receive this blessing, and we left him still unyielding.

"We were received by Mr. Clinton in his very gentlemanly manner, seats being prepared for almost every lady. Yet the Heavenly Stranger, kindest of all friends, still stands knocking at the door of his heart, still, alas! not admitted.

"Mr. Brady, the clerk at Mr. Crothers' saloon, kindly received us, Mr. Crother being still absent. He pleads that this business is the only one he can engage in to support his family decently. 'Better is a little with fear of the Lord than great treasure and trouble therewith. The blessing of the Lord maketh rich, and He addeth no sorrow with it.'

"Mr. Powell—himself a temperate man—still deals out to his fellow men that which has caused so much suffering and misery, because, as he acknowledges, it is a speedier way of making money than by manual labor. 'An inheritance may be gotten hastily at the beginning; but the end thereof shall not be blessed.'

"No meeting was held this afternoon. Although, if we looked at the labors of this day as only the work of men, we might think nothing had been accomplished, we feel strengthened and encouraged to pursue the work to-morrow with renewed diligence. As we came from the different establishments, sometimes with sorrowful hearts because our requests were not granted, we were encouraged by the peals of the church bell telling us that another prayer on our behalf had ascended to the Throne of Mercy.

"When returning from our labors in the evening we are often asked, 'Have you done any good to-day?' It seems strange that those who believe in the promises of God would ask such a question. Methinks had such a question been asked of the children of Israel, on any of those six days in which they surrounded the walls of Jericho, or even during the six times on the seventh day, their answer would have been the words of the Lord to Joshua: 'I have given into thy hand Jericho, and the king thereof, and the mighty men of valor.' These men had neither the Prophets, nor the Gospels, nor the many recorded answers to prayer that God has been granting through all ages down to the present time, to encourage them; yet, by faith, the walls of Jericho fell down after they were encompassed about seven days. Even so, dear friends, shall it be with us. 'He that goeth forth weeping, bearing precious seed, shall doubtless come again with rejoicing, bringing his sheaves with him.'"

"GREENFIELD, O., February 6, 1874.

"This morning we met at the church with our friends in the temperance cause, not to prepare to make our usual daily visits, but to spend the day with them in humble prayer and thanksgiving, for we verily believe the eyes of the Lord are upon us in this place, and He will attend unto our prayers. Hitherto hath He helped us, and He will not forsake his children.

"As we looked over the congregation we saw the face of one here and another there who had been in the bitter bondage of intemperance, but now, with beaming countenance, listening to the words that fell from the lips of our dear friends; and as we knew that the stretched-out arm of Jehovah had redeemed them our hearts swelled with gratitude, and the prayer ascended to God that He would breathe His Holy Spirit upon every part of our nation and send them this blessing.

"And when the morning was past we felt 'Surely the Lord is in this place; this is none other but the house of God and the gate of heaven.'

"During the services a communication from our brethren of the German Methodist Episcopal Church was read before the Temperance Association, and it was incorporated in the report of the League:

GREENFIELD, O., February 4, 1874.

"'At the leaders' meeting of the German Methodist Episcopal Church of this place, the following resolution was passed to rectify the reports that have been circulating in this community, viz.: That all the members of our Church, with the exception of one or two, were against the temperance cause. The pledge that is now circulating in our Church will prove to the the contrary.

"'We, the undersigned ladies of said Church hereby wish to express our feelings and to assure you that we are in perfect harmony with you in striving against this great evil of intoxication, and further pledge ourselves to do all we can in favor of the temperance cause.

"'O. WILKE, Preacher in charge,
"'FREDERICK SCHNARRENBERGER,
"'WILLIAM BUESE,
"'C. M. NEWBECK,
"'H. OSWALD,
"'CHARLES STROBEL.'

"Also, since coming into the church this evening, we have received encouragement from another source:

"'GREENFIELD LODGE, No. 318, F. AND A. M.

"'*To the Ladies of the Temperance League of Greenfield, O.*—*Greeting:*

"'WHEREAS, This lodge has long felt the importance of suppressing the liquor traffic in our midst; and, WHEREAS, The noble women of our town have banded themselves together, and have gone forth, in the strength of Israel's God, to pray for and plead with those engaged in a business that is desolating so many homes to abandon such business; therefore, be it

"'*Resolved*, That we tender our heartfelt sympathy to the ladies of the League engaged in this glorious work of reformation, and hope you will never cease your labor of love until victory perches upon the temperance banner—until there shall not be one place in our town where intoxicating liquor is sold as a beverage.

"'HORACE STRICKLAND, *Secretary.*
"'GREENFIELD, O., *February* 4, 1874.'

"In the afternoon, at the ringing of the bell, we were glad when they said unto us, 'Let us go into the house of the Lord,' still remembering the precious season of this morning.

"Although it had been announced that the services were to be a 'Children's Meeting,' not one of the little bright-eyed types of innocence listened more attentively, nor enjoyed the meeting better, than the old brothers and sisters, the fathers and mothers, or the gray-haired grandfathers and grandmothers; for our Savior said, 'Except ye be converted, and become as little children, ye shall not enter into the kingdom of Heaven.'

"It was a pleasure, too, to know that the saloons of our town were closed with the other business establishments all day, and to have the proprietors come out to church with us as our brethren. 'Oh, that they were wise; that they would understand this; that they would consider their latter end! How should one chase a thousand, and two put ten thousand to flight, except their rock has sold them, and the Lord had shut them up? For their rock is not as our rock, even our enemies themselves being our judges. * * * * Their wine is the poison of dragons and the cruel venom of asps. Is not this laid up in store with me, and sealed up among my treasures? To me belongeth vengeance and recompense; their foot shall slide in due time, for the day of their calamity is at hand, and the things that shall come upon them make haste.'

"KATE DWYER, *Secretary.*"

Men may say what they please about the weakness of being moved by such demonstrations—and those who can keep out of the way do say a great deal; but when one gets into the midst of it and sees old gray-haired mothers and middle-aged matrons pleading with rum-sellers not to ruin their peace and that of the community, it has a telling effect. When kept up a few days the whole community is warmed, the latent sympathy is aroused, and a glow spreads among all classes; the whisky men are soon made to feel that everybody is against them, and unless endowed with a great deal of brute-nerve they fly or yield. It is easy to yield; hard to hold out. It requires immense moral force to withstand a whole community, even when one has the right back of him. But what has the saloon-keeper to fall back upon?

The element of love and good will in this movement makes it a hard thing to fight. One lady at Greenfield remarked on this point:

"We intend to cure this disease by a better treatment that shall not leave a drug disease in the system. Extirpation by law would leave hatreds and jealousies in the community; but prayer and good words leave no sting behind. We don't intend to try legal remedies till prayer and good words are exhausted, and love has lost its power; and we don't intend that shall be until the whole work is accomplished."

And truly there is philosophy in this. Dr. Clinton could not always withstand the prayers and pleadings of good women, his neighbors; he yielded at last, with the best of grace, and now Greenfield is freed from the curse and without any bitter memories to disturb her peace. The ladies there have been earnest in assisting other places, helping on the temperance cause by every means in their power.

New Vienna, a few miles west of Greenfield, was destined to an unpleasant notoriety for a time as the home of "the wickedest man in Ohio." The movement began there the second week in January, and in a week all the saloons were closed but two: one kept by a German woman, named Rice, and the other, a regular "dead-fall" near the depot, by John Calvin Van Pelt. He seemed to hold to predestination, for he swore that all the prayers of all the women in New Vienna would never move him, and that he would "baptize the women if they troubled him again." The next day, when they entered the saloon, they were ordered to leave in so many minutes. Not to be frightened, they commenced their devotional exercises. When the words "May the Lord baptize him with his holy spirit," were spoken, Van Pelt hurled a bucket of filthy water at them, saying: "G—d— you, I'll baptize you." Several buckets of water were thrown, but the ladies heroically stood to their post, although drenched with dirty water. Water failing, beer was thrown, until the ladies were compelled to retire to the outside of the door, where they concluded their devotions. Meanwhile Van Pelt stood at the window, relieving himself of all the filthy epithets known to that class of men. When the procession started to leave the door was thrown open and all invited to come in—that they could have whisky by the pint or half-pint, to suit customers.

Nothing but the intercession of the ladies prevented a mob. Van Pelt was arrested, put in jail, bailed out, then arrested on another charge. He came out again more bitter than ever, and for ten days there was great bitterness in New Vienna. If it had been between men alone, he would either have been killed, or fighting yet; but the whole affair was put under the direction of the ladies, and like all the rest Van Pelt yielded at last. He had become so notorious that when it was rumored about town that he was ready to surrender all the church bells rang merrily, and nearly everybody in town assembled at the "dead-fall." After arriving at his door the women commenced singing, and Van Pelt and several ministers commenced rolling out the whisky, etc., and also the fixtures. Van Pelt then requested that as this was a woman's meeting, and their work, he wished the men to cross the street, with the exception of the ministers, who were allowed to remain. The men consented to his request and left. He then rolled out one barrel of whisky, one barrel of cider, and one keg of beer, and with an ax knocked in the heads of all.

Then, after singing and prayer, he made a few remarks, saying: "Ladies, I now promise you to never sell or drink another drop of whisky as long as I live, and also promise to work with you in the cause with as much zeal as I have worked against you." He also remarked that he hoped the women of the United States would never cease until every drop of whisky was emptied upon the ground as his was.

This was on the 4th of February. Mrs. Rice surrendered the same day, and in one week thereafter Van Pelt was traveling as a temperance lecturer! As a matter of unusual interest I present his first speech, delivered at Hillsboro, February 7th, before the mass temperance convention. First apologizing for the grammatical mistakes that he might make, as he was not an educated man, he spoke as follows:

"The question of the greatest moment to us who are now engaged in this temperance reform is, whether we are working in the right way. Various ways have been tried in the last sixty years, and they have all failed; and why? because there was no heart in them. Men undertook them and failed because they were not sufficiently interested. I believe that these noble women have found the right way, that it is their work, that they are the injured parties, and that they alone can succeed, trusting as they do in the help of Almighty God."

Here Van Pelt answered, in a very satisfactory way, many of the arguments which he had himself used in favor of the business, when he was first visited by the temperance ladies. He then continued as follows:

"How would men proceed if they wanted to dry up the Ohio River? Would not their efforts be directed to drying up the fountains that feed it? Then only would their purpose be accomplished. So it is with you, dear sisters. Although many say that you are not accomplishing much, that you have too great a task before you, don't be discouraged. You are drying up the fountains (now this one, now that) that feed this great river of intemperance. All over our State these fountains are being dried up, and soon your prayers will be answered by an Almighty God, and this great curse will be eternally swept from our land. I am requested by some of these gentlemen to give you some of my experience, but I don't like to do it, for I am ashamed to think how I made these dear sisters suffer. Since I am a changed man, I don't like to speak about it. You all know what a monster I have been pictured; what a hard case I was, almost a demon in human form; what outrageous acts I have done. When these dear sisters called on me first, I looked at this question through the green spectacles of greenbacks, and I endeavored in every manner to drive these brave suffering women away. In addition to my own determination, I had strong inducements offered me to hold out; why, one wholesale whisky man, from Cincinnati, said to me: 'Van Pelt, how much will you take to hold out a year?' I told him that I was a free man, and that I intended to keep free; that I had no price. Why, that man offered to furnish me, free of all charge, all the whisky, wine, and beer that I could sell in Vienna in a year, if I only would hold out. I tell you that man's proposition set me to thinking that their foundations were getting mighty shaky, if they were obliged to offer such inducements. I knew all the time I was doing wrong, but after that, I came to the conclusion that a man who could be hired to do wrong was the meanest kind of a man. I saw myself as my neighbor saw me. Could I be a man, and take the last dime from a drunkard, without seeing the suffering faces of starving children ever before me? I saw myself the monster that I was pictured, and last Monday morning I saw those dear sisters kneeling in the sleet and snow of that terrible day, and heard them offering such fervent prayers for blessings on me, I almost felt that my hand would be paralyzed if ever again I received the drunkard's money, and I dared not longer refuse the visitation of my God. I was conquered then, but I did not give up until a few days later. I tell you, friends, I slept well after that, and now to-day, friends, Vienna is free, and every face you meet is a smiling one; you can feel the working of the Almighty God, and soon I hope that this blessed peace will be all over the land, and the great curse swept away."

During the delivery of this Mr. Van Pelt was frequently applauded. "Hold on, my brother, hold on," was then enthusiastically sung.

Morrow, thirty miles from Cincinnati, at the junction of the Little Miami and Muskingum Valley Railroads, presented probably the most hopeless prospect in Ohio to the crusaders; and the ladies of that place may justly claim the honor of having finished the hardest task of all. In Washington the movement had the advantage of novelty; in other places there was only a limited interest in the liquor business. But Morrow had all the disadvantages of both city and country, and the advantages of neither. Here is the state of facts, existing January 26, when the ladies began their work:

Population, eleven hundred; drinking places, fifteen; increase of population in ten years, two hundred persons; increase of municipal taxation, one hundred and thirty per cent.; decline in business reported at twenty-five per cent.; manufactures nothing, and no increase in the value of property; eighteen vacant dwelling-houses, and numbers of the best citizens removed. Such are the facts given me by the "old and reliable." Verily, it was time for the law or the gospel to do something. The place has a beautiful and romantic site. They have three railroads, and expect connection soon with a trunk line to the East. On one side is the river, and on the other the beautiful hill, with hundreds of sites for palatial residences. In the neighborhood is good fishing and hunting, and all around is scenery unsurpassed in the State of Ohio. Apparently, this is just the place for a favorite summer resort.

Twenty-five years ago Morrow had aspirations. There were, and are, unsurpassed facilities for manufacturing—still unimproved. Three large hotels at that time were filled most of the summer with families and visitors from Cincinnati. The society was good; church, school, and lyceum were thoroughly organized, and, besides the manufacturing interests which were being established, the place expected to become a city of elegant retired country seats. Somehow the saloons got the start, the manufacturers took the alarm, the expected good families did not come, and many that were here moved away. If the place has improved in twenty years, that fact is not apparent to the naked eye. Still there are many good families in Morrow. They have borne the demoralization and tyranny of the whisky power until it has become a question of life and death with them; and they have entered on this struggle in the spirit which patriots fight for their homes; feeling that unless they conquer, they must emigrate. It was not a question of philanthropy alone, and other people's good, here as in some places; they must conquer or die.

The good women entered upon the almost hopeless task, and by incessant labor literally created a healthful public sentiment—it is safe to say that little of it existed before—and in one month had closed two-thirds of the saloons. I visited Morrow soon after the movement was inaugurated, and was witness to many painful and affecting scenes. It seemed to me that the place was whisky-ridden, and sold wholly to Satan; and I could but look upon the praying women as those who labor without hope. But the sequel showed that I had underrated the power in this movement. I was present at a meeting in one saloon, known as the "Blue Goose," kept by a woman. She had several young children, who stood around in open-mouthed wonder—too young to know what it all meant. The ladies completely filled the little "shanty," and after the singing Mrs. J. Graham offered up a fervent prayer. Never was there an orator who more fully realized the situation and fitted the words to the case. It was pre-eminently the prayer of a mother, for a mother, and in the interest of all mothers. As her earnest, pleading petition arose that these children might never suffer from the evils to which they were daily exposed, tears rolled down many faces, and the few revellers who had been surprised in the saloon, withdrew silently, with impressions they can not soon shake off.

At this writing Morrow has but two saloons remaining, both closely besieged, and nearly the entire population have signed the personal pledge. One saloonist obtained a legal injunction against the ladies, of which a particular account is given under the proper heading.

CHAPTER IV.

CAMPAIGN OF DIO LEWIS.

INDICATIONS now pointed toward a national movement in the interests of temperance. Daily papers filled their columns with particular accounts of the work in various places. On a single day the Cincinnati *Commercial* and *Gazette* contained reports, by letter or telegraph, from fifty towns where the movement was in progress. The press of the Eastern cities began to give full details, and commented with various degrees of praise or blame. A few earnest temperance men felt bound to disapprove the methods of the movement, but the majority looked upon it as an opening of Providence for the more rapid regeneration of humanity. Henry Ward Beecher pronounced it "a wonderful religious revival, with a special look toward temperance." Dr. Dio Lewis, by virtue of having first suggested the movement, suddenly found himself in demand. The temperance men of Boston decided to inaugurate the movement in their State, and concluded to begin at Worcester. They called Dr. Lewis to assist them, but he replied that "the best point to fight intemperance in Massachusetts was just now in Ohio." He would come here, devote a few weeks to the work, then return and enter upon a campaign in Massachusetts. With this purpose he came to Cincinnati, having telegraphed the noted Van Pelt to meet him at the Burnet House. There he suggested to the latter that a relation of his experience, and the evils of the liquor traffic, which he knew, by long observation, would be of great advantage to the temperance cause. Van Pelt consented to serve the cause in that way, and a campaign was at once arranged, taking in all points where the movement needed a start or encouragement. Four journalists, representing various Cincinnati papers and the *New York Tribune*, accompanied the two temperance apostles; and the tour was one of great interest.

Xenia was the first point where Dr. Lewis was called upon to show his abilities as an organizer. It was one of the places the crusaders against whisky have hesitated to attack; not that it is exceptionally bad, but it has the two disadvantages—it is a city of eight thousand people, and a rather conservative, aristocratic one. Even among the most sanguine reformers, one often hears this expression: "It will work first-rate in places of two or three thousand, but when they come to the larger cities, they'll be defeated."

An immense audience welcomed the Doctor, and he plunged at once into the subject by stating that he considered this the most important meeting ever held in Xenia. He continued: "I feel a deep anxiety lest the little I have to say shall not be well said, for this movement of the praying women of Ohio has got beyond the direction of any one man; its control belongs only to God." Some startling statements from various judges were then presented, as to the proportion of crimes caused by intoxication, the speaker having the testimony of nineteen eminent jurists, none of whom were temperance men.

In a meeting he had recently attended, a clergyman had recommended the introduction of the light wines of France and Germany to suppress our fiery stimulants; but, said the Doctor, I would not walk across the street to aid any temperance reform that did not plant its two feet square on the rock of total abstinence. [Applause.]

Dr. J. G. Holland had stood for twenty years directly in the path of the temperance reformation of New England by his position on this subject. Said he: "You are not going to work in the right way; men will have stimulants of some kind, the desire for them is as natural as for air and sunlight. In Southern Europe every one drinks his half pint or pint of wine daily, and is the better for it. Let us induce our people to use these stimulants and all will be well." At last Dr. Holland went to Europe, and what did he see? He is a man that prides himself on his consistency. A great deal of his time is taken up in proving that he does not change; that he thinks just as he did seventeen hundred years ago—more or less. But when he got to Southern Europe he took the back track for the first time, so far as I know, in his life. Said he: "God forbid that the drinking customs of my country should be changed for those of this land! Bad as they are there, they are worse here." I too went to Southern Europe, where men use these light wines. And what is the secret of their demoralization there? The women drink!! Every woman as well as every man; and during the time I was there I never heard a woman decline to drink, except because of sickness; and one hour after dinner you could see the effect of wine drinking in the face and eye of every woman of the company! And it is only because the praying mothers and faithful wives of Ohio do not drink that they hate, *loathe*, abbor the *deadly* stuff, that they fight it from their houses as the presence of death, that any such movement as this is possible.

A scathing criticism of moderate drinkers followed. Who, he asked, set the example which young drinkers follow? Evidently not the drunkards, the men who get drunk every time they get the means; for all classes look upon them as disgusting. Nor is it the middle class, who drink habitually and get drunk occasionally; for in every family and social circle you will hear them spoken of thus: "Mr. A. has a good bank account now, but if he goes on this way five years, it won't be so. Mr. B.'s credit is good to-day, but he will be a pauper in ten years if he don't let liquor alone. No; no young man feels called on to imitate them. No; it is the nice, elegant fellows, who turn up delicate cut glasses, and sip the finest foreign wines; or the sturdy, honest old gentleman who takes only pure Bourbon; and the families that keep a little cordial for sociability, or a bottle of brandy in the house "for fear some should be taken suddenly sick in the night!" These are the men who set the fashion, whose every word and motion was imitated. For it is but a few men who set the style for a place; it is but a small number of women who determine the fashion. And there are women, and in the best society, to our shame be it said, who serve as agents to recruit the devil's army of drunkards.

Mrs. Colonel Smith smiles sweetly the first day of January, as she says to the innocent young man who calls, "Take a glass of wine with me before you go." And to that young man she is a very goddess, moving before him in trailing clouds of beauty. The woman who would thus let herself down to be an enlisting officer for the devil's army of drunkards should be tabooed, inexorably shut out from all respectable society forever [Prolonged applause]. A series of interesting sketches followed, showing that the speaker could drop occasionally from the severe to the lively and amusing; but through them all ran the one general moral. There is no safety but in total abstinence, and the moderate drinkers set the example which makes drunkards.

The Doctor gave an exceedingly interesting account of his childhood; that his father died a miserable drunkard, and the town where he resided was being ruined by rum, when the mothers of the place rose in a body and begged, pleaded, and prayed with the rumsellers till the town was cleared of the traffic. He then addressed himself to the question: "What shall be done?"

Nothing had ever raised communities to such a height of moral sublimity as this women's temperance movement of Ohio. Three hundred times, he said, have I given temperance lectures in which I urged this movement, and never found the soil fit for it before. Now that it has come, I almost fear to touch it, lest I hinder. When I saw the women at Morrow praying in front of that saloon, I felt weak—too weak to add anything to the power at work—and I knew then why Brother Van Pelt had surrendered. He must have been half crocodile, half tiger, and all devil to have withstood it. Now friends, the hour of action has come. I propose this plan: We want a chairman, four secretaries, and ten speeches of two or three minutes each by clergymen and leading citizens.

On motion of a citizen, Dr. Lewis himself was unanimously chosen chairman, and Messrs. Dodds, Stein, Colonel Findley, of the Xenia *Gazette*, and Rev. Mr.

Marley, named as secretaries. Short and pointed speeches were then made by Rev. Mr. Bedel, of the Baptist Church, Rev. Mr. Ralston, of the Presbyterian, Rev. J. G. Carson, of the United Presbyterian, Rev. Messrs. Morehead and Starr, Mr. Shaeffer, Rev. Mr. Yockey, and Rev. Marlay. All were enthusiastic in favor of a forward movement; but two expressed doubts as to whether it was quite time for favorable action, and whether the system proposed was the best. At the call for volunteers a hundred and fifty women enlisted for the war.

I left Xenia with the impression that it was too rigidly conservative for the temperance war; a week after I returned and found the city ablaze with excitement. At least five hundred ladies were in the movement, either directly at work or lending assistance to those who were. Every respectable family in the place was represented. The Scotch Seceders, who are numerous there, were peculiarly active. Ladies who had obeyed St. Paul's (supposed) injunction most religiously, now prayed in the streets with the fervor of Methodist exhorters. Ministers who had written elaborately to prove that Christians should sing only the metrical version of the Psalms (in accordance with the creed of that church), now sang a campaign temperance song to the inspiring tune of "John Brown's Body." The wall of separation between the various churches seemed completely broken down. Heretofore the attentive observer, hearing a prayer could distinguish by the tone and style whether it was by a Seceder, Methodist, or other sectarian. But now the nicest ear could not distinguish; all prayed just alike. All seemed as sisters in Christ, and the sanguine were led to hope that this movement would even lead to a complete union between the sects.

I was witness to one most remarkable scene; probably the most thrilling in the course of this movement. On Whiteman street, in a space of six hundred yards, were nine saloons, several of such bad repute that they were known as "Shades of Death,' "Mule's Ear," "Certain Death," "Hell's Half-Acre," and "Devil's Den." Visiting this locality I found five bands of ladies at work. Miss Laura Hicks, teacher, had brought her entire school of young girls to the work for the afternoon, and they were singing in front of Glossinger's saloon. On each side extended a long line of spectators, leaving only a narrow space in the middle of the street. Led by their teacher, the children sang:

"Say, Mr. Barkeeper, has father been here?"

Those familiar with that song will remember that the child is represented as seeking his father through all his usual haunts, and finding him in jail for some offense committed when drunk; that he then intercedes with the jailer, and finally convinces him that it was not his father who committed the offense, but the liquor that drove him wild. There was more than one among the spectators to whom that poetry represented literal fact. Again the children sang; then extracts from Scripture were read, and a lady with a clear, sweet voice offered a fervent prayer :

"O, Lord, our Helper in time of need, we prostrate ourselves in the dust before Thee to beg for the lives of our fathers, our brothers, our sons. O God, help us to save dying men. Help us to rescue the idols of our love. Dying men are all around us; they crowd us in the street; we look upon them in our homes; we shed tears of bitter anguish because we can not save them from this traffic of death. O Lord, our God, consider our tears, our breaking hearts, and send us help to fight this monster of intemperance. How long, O Lord, how long! Must we suffer on and on while we have left the power to suffer. O God, consider the tears of the oppressed; for on the side of the oppressor is power, which Thou alone can crush. Give us, oh! give us back our brothers who are swept away by this torrent of intemperance. Come, dear Lord, and touch the hearts of the dealers in ardent spirits. Send down Thy spirit on this poor man who still turns a deaf ear to our pleading. He will not listen to us. Oh! do Thou soften his heart, that he may know our agony and cease to put evil in the path of those we love. Give us access to the heart of this man. Bless him, O Lord; bless him with the riches of Thy grace. Send Thy ministering Spirit upon him and his family. We know not how to plead as we ought. We know not the way to his heart. Oh! grant that no weak or foolish act of ours may injure the cause of Christ or throw discredit on any good work. Do thou guide and control us; make our weakness strength, and teach us how to pray and labor as we ought. O Lord, our God, wilt Thou not listen to the prayer of those made desolate by rum. Here bowed before Thee are widows, orphans, made such by this traffic—this traffic we must call accursed, for Thou hast cursed it in Thy holy word. O God, withhold the hand of him who would put the bottle to his neighbor's mouth. We feel encouraged to labor on against this traffic which we know Thou hast condemned. Oh, teach us how to work and give us the victory. Grant that the rule of temperance and law may be set up, and that righteousness may flow as a river and the knowledge of God cover the whole earth. Then will our sons no longer fall before those who lie in wait for their souls; then will our daughters no longer mourn because of the traffic in rum. And bring us all, both the dealer in rum and those who fall by the traffic, to see more clearly the light of Thy truth, and finally unite us at Thy right hand, we ask for Jesus' sake, Amen."

Again the children sang, and while the crowd of some hundreds slowly dispersed, different ladies read extracts from the Scriptures. All this time a plump and healthy looking German woman sat at an upper window in the besieged house and looked down with indifference upon the ladies. Sometimes she held up her youngest child for him to take a look at the scene, and again laughed and nodded to acquaintances over the way. She was not even sufficiently interested to get angry.

I had just returned to the hotel after this scene when I heard a great shout in the street, and soon after all the church bells in the city commenced ringing. At the same time there arose a prolonged cheering from the Grangers' Convention, just across the street from the hotel, and it was evident that something unusual had happened. Going out, I saw crowds of people thronging toward Whiteman street, and heard on every hand in joyful accent, "The 'Shades of Death' has unconditionally surrendered." The good news proved true, and I found Whiteman street thronged with people. At a little before 3 o'clock, as it appeared from the general account, Mr. Steve Phillips, proprietor of the "Shades of Death," invited the ladies to enter, and announced that he gave up every thing to them, and would never sell anything intoxicating in Xenia again. Then the ladies, joined by the spectators, sang "Praise God, from whom all blessings flow," while the liquors were rolled into the street. A half barrel of blackberry brandy, the same of highwines, a few kegs of beer, and some bottles of ale and whisky were soon emptied into the street, amid the shouts of an enthusiastic multitude. The leading lady then announced that if Mr. Phillips went into any other business in Xenia they should feel it a duty to support him; a dispatch was sent to the Grangers, eliciting three cheers, and all the bells were set ringing in honor of the first great victory. When I arrived the liquor had mostly collected in one depression in the street, and such a stench went up, "a rank offense, that smelt to heaven," as made me think it a very fortunate thing for somebody's stomach that the liquor had been poured out. Of the women around, some were crying, some laughing, a few alternately singing and returning thanks. One elderly lady in the edge of the crowd was almost in hysterics, but still shouting in a hoarse whisper such as one often hears at camp meeting: "Bless the Lord! O-o-o, bless the Lord." She had the appearance of a lady in good circumstances, and a citizen informed me that she is ordinarily one of the quietest, most placid of women. One of her sons died of intemperance, and another is much addicted to liquor. On every side nothing was witnessed but smiles, laughter, tears, prayers, hand-shakings, and congratulations.

The "Shades of Death" was considered by the temperance party as the "back-bone of the rebellion," and within twenty-four hours four more saloons had surrendered. The movement continues with unabated vigor, and only twelve saloons remain. Twenty-nine have been closed.

From Xenia the apostles of temperance, accompanied by the journalists, went to Springfield. On the evening of February 11th sixteen hundred people crowded the Opera House to its utmost capacity. On the stand were "Mother Stewart," Rev. Mr. Bennett and other ministers of the city, Mr. Clifton Nichols, editor of the *Republic*, and the representatives of five journals. Mr. Nichols, the Chairman, stated that Dr. Lewis desired them to hear Mr. Van Pelt give an account of his "closing day" in New Vienna. That gentleman advanced to the front and plunged at once *in medias res*. He gave a lengthy account of his feel ings as the ladies came day after day; told what his legal advisers said to him, but "thanked God that he took the turn of his own mind, and let them legal gentlemen take their own course."

"Now the men outside had tried various means to make me surrender, but it warn't a bit of use. When I told the ladies I would decide, I saw them coming down the street, funeral file, that afternoon. I never had anything come over me like that—coming to pray for I, that had dealt out that that ruined 'em to their fathers and brothers and sons. I couldn't ask more to know they was sincere. I turned to Brothers Winter and Hill and said, 'Will you carry out the whisky?' I never seed such a look as they give me. I reckon they thought I was jestin'; but for all that they was mighty willin'. * * * * * And when the whisky run out there went up such a shout as I never heern before and never expect to agin. And there were such faces—more nearer to angel faces than I ever expect to see till I stand in the presence of God. There was old man Hill, and old man Johnson, that hadn't shed a tear, I reckon, for ten years, cried like children; and they hugged me and cried; and everybody was happy because the last whisky shop in Vienna had surrendered. And we all said God was in it, and the movement never would stop till all the whisky shops was driv' out of the State."

Everybody laughed encouragingly at the young convert's idiomatic English; then Dr. Lewis gave a somewhat startling discourse, on "pure and drugged liquors." He did not sympathize with the wish for pure liquors; on the contrary, he considered the poison compounder the friend of temperance. He did not know of any drug so deadly that it would not improve whisky. He would bid the mixers God speed, if it be lawful to use the name of God in such a connection. There is no nonsense so pervading and injurious as this talk about unadulterated liquors. Men say, "O, if we only had the pure liquors that our grandfathers had, we would live on as they did; it is this poison stuff that kills us off." It is all nonsense. The reason liquor hurts us worse than our grandfathers is the difference in other physical conditions. They worked hard in the open air, lived on coarse food, and though they drank often, did live out three-fourths of their days. The men who live in the open air now, who start with a good constitution and unusual physical advantages, can live as long. Be not deceived. Alcohol is poison—*it is poison—it is poison!* The more deadly it can be made the better. If a man has become a habitual drinker, the sooner he dies the less harm he does. Is it not better for him to go in a year or two, than to go on a curse to himself and the world for twenty? If the whisky could be so mixed that it would kill a man in three days, it would be a glorious thing for temperance.

This radical doctrine somewhat astonished the audience, and was savagely criticized by the press; but the Doctor stoutly maintains the correctness of his position. After the Doctor several persons made short speeches. I only present entire that of "Mother Stewart," as she is a sort of pioneer in the cause:

"God seems to be giving us the desire of our hearts, but we have a very peculiar warfare here. I can not describe it. We never did anything until we started to work at the saloons. It seemed to me that we were only beating the air. Four months have passed since that poor woman came to me for help for herself and children against the rumsellers that were killing her husband. I told her to-day to come here to-night, and see if this meeting gave her hope; and she is in the audience. At last the people are interested; some actual drunkards, and young men, drinkers but not yet drunkards, have taken my hand and said to me, 'Go on, Mother Stewart; we do hope you will succeed.' Sometimes I have felt so discouraged I almost wished that God would lay me on a bed of sickness, for I might be an obstacle in the way of reform. Still we worked on. I felt when that poor woman came to me, that our great reliance must be in prayer. The great question was—could we succeed in that way in this city? At last we went forth, and then a host of friends seemed to spring out of the ground. The burden of this thing has been on my mind till I have felt that I could not live unless we went forward. We could not trust to other causes. The politicians admit that they are powerless. They are so entangled that they can not act.

"On Monday two or three went out and prayed. Good women came and prayed with us, and at last, yesterday, we went to the saloons, twenty or thirty of us, and to-day more came—yes, seventy or eighty, and you all know the result. Many gentlemen have said to me, 'Those places must be closed,' but I felt almost in despair when I received a telegram from Dr. Lewis. As our band increased there was a great crowd of men and boys, but they were very polite and respectful. They only seemed anxious to see and hear. To-day we visited the Lagonda House saloon; the proprietor treated us very kindly, but locked the outside door to keep the crowd out. He gave us the billiard rooms, and we had a very precious season there. At the next place I tried to talk a crowd collected. The man came out and said, 'Get away, get away, every one of you; I don't want any trespassers; you shan't stand on my steps.' But I was never more composed. When I started down from the porch a hundred voices said, 'Stay where you are.' 'Go on, Mother Stewart, go on.' Then a policeman took the man in, and when we were ready to leave, he came out in good humor and bid us good day."

A gentleman of rather quiet style afterward said on this subject:

"If that fellow had touched one hair of Mother Stewart's gray head, his house would have been leveled to the ground."

There is nothing more curious in the phenomena of the movement than the general respect, amounting almost to love or hero worship, which some of the worst rummies and saloonists feel for the good ladies engaged. "Mother" Stewart has warm friends among the worst people in Springfield.

Short and pithy speeches were made by General Keifer, Rev. Mr. Bennett, Rev. Mr. Spring, L. H. Olds, A. R. Ludlow, Rev. Mr. Seaver, and Rev. Mr. Dutton. A regular organization was then perfected. The work still goes on in Springfield, and the ladies are confident of final success; but there have been few surrenders, and many hindrances. This was the first trial in a city of more than eight thousand people; and it seems to show that the difficulties in every large city will be very great. In such there are saloonatics enough to keep each other in countenance; they have a business association and society of their own, and by alliances with political parties and social circles they are imbedded in the very structure of society, and it is like cutting out a cancer to remove them—the wound will be deep and the process dangerous.

A greater difficulty is a lack of unity in other parties; there is too much diversity of interests. Men do not get so close together and know each other so well as in the country places. If all the temperance men could be drawn to one side and make a fair attack on the saloonatics, they would gladly do so; but each man fears that in striking at them he is striking at his neighbor and indirectly at himself.

But the greatest difficulty is with the ladies themselves, and their natural tendency not to unite. In a small place all respectable ladies are in one social order; church and society blend insensibly, and it is comparatively easy to unite the good women for any good object. But in a city there are scores of cliques, circles, and social strata. Eminently respectable people in one circle do not know equally respectable people in another; and nearly all women are afraid of nearly all other women, until they get pretty well acquainted. All true women shrink from publicity or open manifestations of the emotions; and for obvious reasons those in a city much more than those in the country, who are known to all they are likely to meet. So much for human calculation; but a cause may be so important, and acquire such momentum, that it will sweep in all ladies of all the social strata. In that case, Springfield, according to her population, will have a thousand ladies at work instead of a hundred, and her saloons can then be closed just as surely as the rum-holes of Washington or New Vienna.

From Springfield the temperance missionaries went down to Lebanon, where a sort of legal fight was in progress. The temperance men—no women taking part—had employed a Cincinnati detective who put in one week in Lebanon, and got evidence enough to close all the saloons by law but one. It was a bad time then to inaugurate the Women's Movement, nevertheless they determined to try it. Eight hundred people filled Washington Hall, among them a delegation from Shaker Village. Van Pelt dramatized his conversion and surrender, to the intense delight of the audience. Lewis incited to immediate action. Ten minute speeches were made by Rev. Burroughs. Dr. Byers, Rev. Clark, Rev. Roberts, Rev. Sprole, Messrs. Fox, Holbrook, Crothers, Kinsey. Wilson, Judge Keys, Graham, and D. B. Van Pelt, of the Normal School. The audience voted unanimously, by a rising vote, to sustain the ladies in any move they decided upon, with moral support and money; and the movement was regularly organized. But the love-cure *after* the law-cure did not work well; too much ill-feeling had been excited, but at the end of three weeks' work the Secretary of the Temperance League sends us this report :

"LEBANON, O., February 27, 1874.

"Legal prosecutions began about January 4, and the women's movement February 14, with one hundred and fifty women now at work. Two saloons have closed, and one drug store has signed the pledge. One saloon and two drug stores are still at work. Though the pledge has just been started, six hundred have signed."

Thence we crossed to Franklin, on the C. C. C. & I. Road ("Dayton Short Line"), where the women had already prayed six saloons out of town, and were at work on the seventh and last. It is an old-fashioned "water-rats'" retreat, on the bank of the canal, kept by a Mr. Monger, who bids fair to become notorious as the only white man in Ohio who is unmoved by prayers, tears, or entreaties. He still holds out, and will, probably, until the law shuts up his saloon, as it is now likely to do.

Miss Sarah Butler, of Franklin, has achieved almost a national reputation by her labors in the temperance cause. Mr. Handy, of the New York *Tribune*, in our party, was so struck with the prayer she uttered in front of Monger's saloon that he telegraphed it entire to the *Tribune*. I heard her afterward, at the State Convention, give a simple account of their labors in Franklin; and, when she concluded, in that audience of twelve hundred people, I think there were not a score of eyes free from tears. So wonderful is the eloquence of pure, unaffected nature, when pleading in a good cause.

The Doctor and Mr. Van Pelt then visited Marysville and Mt. Vernon, where the work was started and is being prosecuted with great vigor. At Delaware, our party was re-united. The Doctor was invited there by the *Chi Phi*, one of those mysterious Greek-letter fraternities which abound in colleges. Finding that there was no temperance organization, and that he was invited merely as a lecturer, Dr. Lewis put it to a vote whether he should proceed on his regular plan. The audience voted for temperance. The Doctor was made chairman, as usual, and Messrs. M. D. Coville, Cyrus Pratt, and Dr. Merrick named as an advisory committee.

Dr. Lewis gave a short address, and the organization was soon perfected. The large audience filling Williams' Opera-house was responsive and enthusiastic. Short speeches were made by Rev. Voght, Mr. Handy, of the New York *Tribune*, Rev. Crook, President Richardson, of the Female College, Mr. McDowell, Professor LaCroix, Professor Whitlock, Professor Perkins, Professor Gardner, Drs. Welch and Barnes. The men voted unanimously to sustain the women in their work, and the latter decided, without a dissenting vote, to organize. In less than twenty-four hours from the time the movement began, there were a hundred ladies upon the streets at work.

In the meantime a preliminary mass meeting had been held at Columbus, and a call issued for the State Temperance Convention, of which account is given elsewhere. Our tour with the temperance apostles closed appropriately with a day of rejoicing, at Washington C. H., where the movement began. On the 17th of February, our party of half a dozen journalists and as many temperance apostles, reached that place at noon. Almost the entire population, headed by a band, escorted the Doctor to Music Hall, where a formal reception took place. On the platform, besides the Doctor and representatives of the press, were the various ministers of the place, the officers of the Ladies' League, and prominent citizens.

Dr. Lewis was called, and came forward amid loud cheers, when the address of welcome was pronounced by Mrs. M. G. Carpenter:

"DR. LEWIS—In the name of the women of Washington I welcome you. Eight weeks ago, when you first came among us, you found us a people of willing hearts and generous impulses, fully alive to the evils of intemperance, but needing the magnetism of a master mind to rouse us into a determined resistance to its ravages. Yours was that mind. Your hand pointed out the way. You vitalized our latent activities. You roused us all, men and women together, and we have gone forth to the battle side by side, as God intended we should; ourselves perfect weakness, but God mighty in strength. He has given the success—not yet complete, 'tis true, but our faith is still unshaken. He sent you here; He put the thought into your head; He prepared our hearts to receive it; He has directed our steps. And now He has brought you among us again to gladden you with the fruition of hope long deferred—to see the seed, sown long ago by your mother, springing up, budding, and bearing fruit. Dr. Lewis, in behalf of this whole people, I again welcome you to the hearts and homes of Washington."

The Doctor replied with great feeling:

"MADAME AND FRIENDS—I can not make a speech on this occasion. I may, perhaps, compare myself to an Indian on a visit to the city of Washington—from the frontier to the place where the battle has long been fought and won. I have always been on the frontier, always engaged in the battle of reform, and now, to find anything really done, to find a town positively free from the curse of liquor-selling, it seems that there is nothing for me to do. I feel as one without his working harness. But I will say this: None but God can ever know how much I owe to this town, nor how fortunate it was for me and for many that I came here. I will not not say that this is the only community in which the work could be begun. The heroism and self-sacrifice displayed in other places, the moral force developed in Southern Ohio, would make such a remark invidious. Often have I tried to start this movement. Once in particular, in one of the most moral towns in New England. Two United States Senators came upon the platform to give the movement their sanction. We had as fine an audience as could be assembled, and I said to myself, 'At last we are going to succeed.' But it was a dead failure. I know not why. All the elements of success seemed to be there; but some invisible force was lacking. There is an invisible force at work in this movement. At last I came to you, and you delighted me by your work. You come out to meet me with music and words of welcome. But I come to thank you, to take you by the hands, to look into your eyes, and tell you how much I owe to you for being the first to cheer me with success. I am indebted to you for bringing out this plan. I am indebted to you a thousand times more than you are to me. But the hour of victory leaves me with little to say. I have never been able to visit the battle-fields after victory—have always gone on to new fields. I can only close by tendering you my earnest thanks."

After witnessing for a day the rejoicing of the people of this redeemed town, the Organizer of the movement went to Springfield, where also he received an ovation. He also viewed the battle-ground at Hillsboro, and thence went to Columbus. Immediately after the close of the State Convention, he went East to assist in organizing the movement there, and on the 17th of March was to return and work in Ohio "as long as he can do any good."

CHAPTER V.

A STATE ORGANIZATION IN OHIO.

THE great mass meeting in the interest of the Women's Temperance Movement held in the City Hall, Columbus, on Monday, February 16th, did only one thing of importance; and that was to call a State Convention to be held in the same place eight days later. This action of the meeting was announced to the public in the following card from Dio Lewis:

"CALL FOR A CONVENTION.

"At an immense meeting in the City Hall, Columbus, Ohio, it was voted to call a convention of the friends of the 'Women's Temperance Movement,' to meet in that Hall on Tuesday, February 24, at 2 P. M.

"General consultation, and the establishment of a bureau, are the objects of the convention. The bureau will supply lecturers and organizers. In brief, it will supply the conditions of success.

"Every city, town, village, and neighborhood in the State is invited to send delegates. Half of them should be women. If the towns where the movement is already in progress would send those who have had most experience in the work, it would prove an important contribution.

"It is believed that a more important convention has never been called in the State.

"In the event of the failure of any community to send delegates, any earnest temperance workers from such community will be welcomed to the conference.

"Persons accustomed to public speaking, who would consent to serve in organizing the movement in various localities, are invited to attend the convention. Your obedient servant,

"DIO LEWIS.

A STATE ORGANIZATION IN OHIO. 61

On the appointed day Columbus was enlivened by the presence of temperance workers, male and female, from all parts of the State where there was any interest in the movement, and it was evident from the start that the convention was to be largely attended and result in great good. Many of the delegates spent the morning in communion with the ladies of Columbus at a prayer meeting in the Town Street Church. Here great enthusiasm was manifested. Dio Lewis directed the proceedings with even more than his usual tact and ability, and excellent speeches were made by Mrs. Dessellum, of Columbus; Mrs. Stewart, of Cedarville; Miss Kate Dwyer, of Greenfield; Mrs. Lewis, of Columbus; Mrs. W. E. Strong, of New Lexington; Mrs. M. McC. Brown, of Alliance; and others.

The session of the State Convention began in the City Hall at 2 o'clock P. M. The large auditorum was nearly filled with delegates, of whom a large majority were ladies. The reporters estimated the entire number of persons present at twelve hundred. The assemblage was called to order by Rev. W. B. Chadwick, of Columbus, on whose motion Dr. Dio Lewis was called to the chair. Cliff. M. Nichols, of the Springfield *Republic*, and Rev. Mr. Badgely were elected Secretaries.

Dr. Lewis invited all ministers and editors on the platform, and about thirty accepted the invitation. Mother Stewart, of Springfield, was then escorted to the stand and offered a fervent prayer for the blessing of God upon the deliberations of the convention, and upon every effort in the cause of temperance. The assembly then arose and sung "All hail the power of Jesus' name," with fine effect.

Dr. Lewis invited the delegations, from all places

where the women's war had been carried on, to send their most active workers upon the platform, and some fifty ladies came forward.

On motion, a Committee on Permanent Organization was named, consisting of five ladies and three gentlemen: Mrs. Eliza Thomson, Chairman; Mrs. Mary Brown, Mrs. Conway, of Cedarville; Mrs. B. T. Custer, of London; Mrs. McCabe, of Delaware; and Messrs. Stewart, Gardner, and Keen.

The following were named a Committee on Resolutions: Mother Stewart, Chairman; Mrs. Lizzie T. McFadden, of Cadiz; Mrs. M. W. Barnes, of Springfield; Mrs. Lowe, of Xenia; Mrs. Dr. Sharpe, of London; Mrs. Sarah Pollard, of Columbus; and Messrs. C. M. Nichols, H. S. Fullerton, and J. M. Richmond.

The Committee retired, and the Chairman called for "volunteer speakers—old workers in the cause." The first call was for Mr. Van Pelt, who came on the stand and spoke very briefly. One delegation sent forward Mrs. Timmons, of Clarksburg, Ohio, who gave account of the work there.

After singing, Mrs. Laura C. Findlay, of Xenia, addressed the convention, making a report of the work in that city, from its beginning. Her speech was followed by the singing of "Glory, glory, hallelujah!"

The Chairman read a dispatch from Lancaster, stating that the women, one thousand strong, were at work; that prayer was their watchword, and they proposed to "fight it out on that line." [Applause.] Dr. Lewis said this was good news, and proposed three hearty cheers, which were given.

Mr. T. W. Tallmadge read a letter from Mrs. William I. Reese (sister of General Sherman), expressing regret that circumstances prevented her from accepting an invitation to be present at the convention, and expressing warm sympathy with the movement.

The Committees being still in retirement, Dr. Lewis called for speeches from the ladies. The speeches were so full of the spirit of the movement, and contained so many facts of interest, that we can not refrain from putting their substance on permanent record.

Miss Sewell had been engaged in this cause for years past. What she had seen lately repaid her for all her labor. She was truly glad her eyes had ever beheld this movement. God surely is in the work. It is a religious movement. Long have governments tried by legislation to subdue the rum-seller. Her theory for years had been that through prayer success would come. Her sisters might feel disposed to speak of their weakness, but by trusting in Jesus they would receive strength to subdue the hearts of the most wicked men engaged in this work of death. These men know and feel that it is the sin of sins in which they are engaged, and it only wants the attention and faith and prayers of pious mothers and sisters, offered up at a throne of Heavenly Grace, to subdue their hearts. Some people called this Dio Lewis' movement. It is not his. It is God's work. God is in it, and it will go forward.

Miss Kate Dwyer, of Greenfield, said the Lord had done great things for us, whereof we are glad. We commenced the work somewhat differently in our place from that pursued in other towns. We sent a note to every liquor-seller in the place—of which there were fifteen—requesting them to meet us the next morning, the druggists at one church, and the saloon-keepers at another. One druggist met the ladies and signed the pledge. That was the only one that met us.

But there was one saloon-keeper who sent us word

that he would have been with us, but was detained at home by sickness in his family. He sent us word, however, to bring the pledge to him, and he would sign it. We went to him with the pledge. He signed it, and with tears in his eyes begged us to pray for him. He said we knew he had a praying mother.

The latter part of the same week we visited one of the hotels where there was a saloon, and asked the keeper to sign the pledge. His child came into the room where we were and putting her arms around her father's neck, said, "Oh pa, please sign the pledge." He pushed her from him, saying, "Go away my child, you do not understand it; I will tell you about it after while." Said she, "Oh, pa, *do* sign it?" That night he had a dance, participated in by the very lowest persons in the village. He had other liquor sellers to come and play on instruments of music, and the playing and dancing were kept up the whole night. We could hear them quite plainly from our house. Some of our friends seemed much discouraged in regard to his case. That man at one time had been a follower of our dear Savior, but he seemed now so far gone that there was little hope for him. The next day we met at the church for prayer before starting out on our mission, and afterward, when returning from one of the saloons, a gentleman met us and said this man, to whom I have just referred, desired us to call there and receive his signature to the pledge. When we entered the place he met us with tears in his eyes, and said: "God bless you, ladies, that you ever came here. I thank you for it." He took us in the room, and said: "Here on this counter where I have sold liquor I will now sign the pledge." He signed it, and said: "Here, ladies, I will take down these bottles, and right where

I have filled them I will place the family bible, and every morning I will invoke God's blessing upon us."

Friends, you ought to see that man since that. He does not look like the same man. Before that when he met us he would hold down his head. Now he meets us with a smile, and always seems glad to meet us.

Miss Dwyer also referred to a woman who kept a saloon in the village, who, through their influence, quit the business, was converted and joined the church, and related other successes that had attended their labors.

Miss Butler, of Franklin, said the friends of temperance have met in our place every week for three years, and asked God to bless the temperance cause. When we heard of the work our sisters were doing at Hillsboro we felt that we must take hold of this work as they were doing. For five weeks we have labored in this way, and intend to continue until every saloon in the place is closed.

"God has led us on in this work. I thank Him that I live in this day, and that I have been permitted to engage in this great work, because it has done me so much good. These five weeks have been the happiest weeks of my life."

She gave an account of an instance where a saloon-keeper had employed some men to furnish the music for a dance he intended to have. When these musicians appeared the ladies were engaged in singing and praying in front of the saloon. These men were so affected by the scene that they told the saloonist they did not think that playing and dancing and singing and praying were intended to go together, and they went away and had no dance.

Said she, "God is in this movement, and has drawn together the hearts of Christian women as never before. The time was when our Presbyterian friends thought women should not pray in public, and it was very easy to tell the difference between the prayers of Presbyterians and Baptists and Methodists. But now they all pray alike." [Laughter and applause.]

They had succeeded in closing all the saloons in their village but one, and felt that the keeper of that could not much longer resist their pleadings. They were determined never to give up till the work was accomplished.

After the speeches the Committee on Nominations made their report, and the following officers were elected:

PRESIDENT—Mrs. H. C. McCabe, of Delaware.

VICE-PRESIDENTS—Mrs. Eliza J. Thompson, Hillsboro; Mrs. Rosa Stewart, Cedarville; Mrs. M. G. Carpenter, Washington C. H.; Mrs. Amanda Clark, Newark; Miss Kate Dwyer, Greenfield; Mrs. Rev. Wyant, Mt. Vernon; Mrs. Rev. Dr. Hatfield, Cincinnati; Mrs. John Walker, Logan; Mother Stewart, Springfield; Mrs. Rev. Runyan; Mrs. Z. T. Walker, Marietta; Mrs. General Ewing, Lancaster; Mrs. Granville Moody, Ripley; Miss Kate Shallcross, Gallipolis; Miss Virginia Copeland, Zanesville; Mrs. Shurr, Bellefontaine; Mrs. L. C. Allen, Tiffin; Mrs. E. C. McVilly; Mrs. Judge Mayo, McArthur; Miss Rebecca Rice (Professor in Antioch College), Yellow Springs; Mrs. Joseph Cloakey, Middletown; Miss Henrietta Moore, Marion; Mrs. Rev. William Jones, Findlay; Mrs. David Spangler; Mrs. Brown, Athens; Mrs. Hortensia Beeman, New Lexington; Miss Maggie Beattie, Ashland; Mrs. A. W. Swapel, Dayton; Mrs. William Herr.

SECRETARY—Miss Kate Gardner, of Columbus.

TREASURER—Mrs. Mary Brum, of Columbus.

EXECUTIVE COMMITTEE—Mrs. Maria Bates, Mrs. R. A. S. Janney, Mrs. A. E. Tremaine, Mrs. L. Dessellum, and Mrs. Joan Galloway, all of Columbus.

ADVISORY COMMITTEE—Mr. A. A. Stewart, Hon. Chauncey N Olds, and Hon. E. E. White, all of Columbus.

It was resolved, on motion of Rev. W. B. Chadwick,

A STATE ORGANIZATION IN OHIO.

that the Association should be known as the "Women's Temperance Association of Ohio;" and on the recommendation of the Committee on Resolutions the following declaration of principles was adopted unanimously by a rising vote:

Resolved, That the success of the Ohio women's movement in behalf of temperance reform has given us substantial assurance that the traffic in and use of intoxicating drinks can and will be removed from the State and Nation.

Resolved, That in the prosecution of this work we rely on Divine assistance, secured through fervent, persistent, and importunate prayers to Almighty God, offered in faith in the Lord Jesus Christ, and with hearts filled with love for souls.

Resolved, That faithful and persistent prayer must, as an inevitable result, be accompanied by efficient personal and organized work.

Resolved, That in addition to contributions of money, generously and freely given, it is recommended that the men aiding the women's effort to suppress intemperance in our communities, and to the women who carry on the work, to avoid all envy, hatred, malice, and all uncharitableness, all bitterness of speech and denunciation of the men engaged in the liquor traffic, to cultivate their acquaintance and kindly feeling, and by all honorable and practicable means to assist them in changing from a business injurious to society, to some other, remunerative to themselves, and beneficial to the community.

At the night session of the convention Senator Goodhue presided, by request of Dr. Lewis, and the opening prayer was offered by Rev. M. S. Carpenter, of Washington C. H. Van Pelt made another speech, and interesting remarks were also made by Miss Moore, of Morrow, Mrs. Eliza Thompson, of Hillsboro, Miss Stone, of Marietta, Rev. M. W. Hamma, of Springfield, and Rev. W. M. Grimes, of Cadiz.

Dr. Lewis took this occasion to make a personal explanation at the request of friends. It had been reported that he was traveling about praying at fifty dollars a night. He had been at the West about two weeks, laboring as he had never before labored in his life, having managed nineteen meetings, to say nothing of the work of the present meeting. During that time he had received $315. After paying his expenses—including the expenses of telegraphing, sometimes amounting to ten dollars a day—he would have left less than half of what he had been in the habit of receiving for a single lyceum lecture. [Applause.] Dr. Lewis then made some interesting suggestions as to how active operations should be begun and carried on in cities as well as towns. He also replied to numerous questions from the audience.

All accounts agree that this convention was a most harmonious body, and that its sessions were both interesting and beneficial. The Executive Committee now constitute a bureau which may be of great use in giving sugestions as to the conduct of the movement in collecting reports of progress, and in supplying speakers and organizers. The address of this bureau is thus given: "The Bureau of the Women's Temperance Movement, Columbus, Ohio.

CHAPTER VI.

LEGAL OBSTACLES—THE DECISION OF JUDGE SMITH.

AT the date of this writing no serious legal obstacles have been met by the women of Ohio, except at Hillsboro and at Morrow. The history of the Hillsboro case has been given as fully as necessary in another chapter. The decision of Judge Steele is not published because it bears only upon technical points, and does not affect the main questions at issue between the women and the liquor dealers. The case was ably argued, however, and but for the length of the speeches we would gladly publish what was said on either side.

The Morrow case is more interesting, because the decision seems to establish definitely the right of the people to suppress a public nuisance in the mode adopted by the women of Morrow and other towns in dealing with saloon-keepers. The following is a statement of the case with a full report of the able decision rendered by Judge Smith:

On the 17th of February, one Henry Scheide, a saloon-keeper of Morrow, in a hearing before Judge Gilmore, of Eaton, obtained a temporary injunction against the following named persons:

Mrs. E. R. Grim,	Mrs. H. J. Coffeen,
Frank Forshnell,	Josiah Fairchild,
Geo. W. Davis,	Porter Corson,
John Hanford,	Jas. H. Jeffery,
Oscar T. Hanford,	W. P. Hanford,
B. F. Wilson,	J. T. Welch,

Mrs. J. E. Roof,
  John P. Kibbey,
  Richard Green,
  Geo. Hurner,
  Jos. H. Ludlow,
  Thos. Smith,
  Christ. Scherrer,
  Jas. Goodpaster,
  Wm. A. Staley,
  A. Green,
  Henry Hayner,
  Jas. Wilkerson,
  Jackson Abery,
  W. Vandervort,
  Jos. Vandervort,
  L. Goepper,
  J. Cummins,
  T. J. Baker,
  H. Clevenger,
  E. Cadwallader,
  G. S. J. Brown,
  John T. Roach,
  Jonah Stubbs,
  Runyon,
  Gustin,
Misses Lissie Dugan,
  N. Thompson,
  Carrie Wager,
  Susie Watkins,
  Lois Clevenger,
  A. Goodpaster,
  Lizzie Green,
  Ettie Fairchild,
  Clara Goepper,
  Nettie Snider,
  Anna Mounts,
  Louisa Beeler,
  J. Thompson,
  Luella Roach,
  Hattie Fairchild,

Mrs. B. T. Ready,
  Wm. P. Mounts,
  F. Cunningham,
  John Simonton,
  John Roosa,
  Jas. L. Tuck,
  Thos. Miranda,
  Wm. Gilhan,
  Jacob Snyder,
  Perry Carson,
  S. H. Brant,
  Jas. Dynes.
  Geo. Brant,
  W. T. Mounts,
  John Dunn,
  A. W. Cadwallader,
  Joseph Baker,
  Hiram Cadwallader,
  W. G. Hopkins,
  J. Robinson,
  P. Coudon,
  G. W. Starkey,
  Hadley,
  Melvina Davis,
  Elmira Howard,
Misses Adie Starkey,
  Clara Bailey,
  Lilie Clevenger,
  M. Clevenger,
  Nancie Guthrie,
  Belle Mounts,
  Cynthia Lloyd,
  Mary Goepper,
  Elida Ebery,
  H. G. Moore,
  Olive Coffeen,
  Lena Thompson,
  Minnie Quick,
  Nettie Roosa,
  Anna Fairchild,

Misses Ida Getz,   Misses Mary Snider,
    Eliza Grim,   Anna Grim,
    Emma Snider,   L. Clevenger,
    Nancy Gleehan,   Clara Dynes,
    Martha Dynes,   Ida Dugan,
    Mara Fairchild,   Mattie Koogle.

AND THE FOLLOWING GENTLEMEN:

George S. J. Browne,   Wm. T. Whitacre,
Benjamin F. Wilson,   J. E. Roop,
J. W. Stubbs,   Lewis Fairchild,
Josiah Fairchild,   Thomas Smith,
George Hurner,   Rev. Wm. Young,
J. C. Dynes,   Lee Cummins,
Wm. Zimmer,   Dr. Dio Lewis,
             J. C. Van Pelt.

The following is a copy of the petition presented by Henry Scheide, and the one upon hearing which Judge Gilmore granted the temporary injunction on the above-named persons:

"The said Henry Scheide, plaintiff, prays that each and every one of the said defendants, individually, jointly, and collectively, be restrained, prohibited, and enjoined from molesting, disturbing, or hindering the said Henry Scheide in the prosecuting and conducing his said business, upon any pretense or pretext whatever, and invading or meeting in or about his premises to obstruct his said business; and also prays judgment against all of said defendants for the sum of one thousand dollars, and prays for all other proper relief in the premises."

The trial of the women and their aiders and abettors took place in Lebanon, before Judge Smith. Counsel for the plaintiff—O'Neil, of Lebanon, and Wallace and Mayor Scantlin, of Morrow. The defendants' counsel were Ex-Lieutenant Governor McBurney, General Durbin Ward, and Messrs. Probasco and Van Harlingin, of Lebanon, and Cunningham, of Morrow. The interest of the people of Warren county in the decision of the case was shown by the unparalleled attendance on the session of the court while it was under consideration. A correspondent says the whole town of Morrow came over and emptied itself upon Lebanon. Forty women included in the list of defendants were among the crowd. These became the special guests of the Lebanon ladies, who gave them a public dinner. These forty marched from the church to the court-house in solemn procession. The excitement was intense in the town, and the case the only topic of conversation. The court-house was built with the intention of accommodating about one-half the number that squeezed in on this occasion. The crowd occupied first the seats intended for the public, then they encroached upon the space reserved for the lawyers, and finally they inserted themselves behind the bar, and sat along side of Judge James M. Smith, who presided in this case as chancellor.

The argument of counsel on either side was able. After patiently hearing all that was to be said, Judge Smith took the case under consideration, and on the 7th of March announced his decision as follows:

"On the 17th day of February a temporary injunction was allowed in this case by Judge Gilmore, restraining the defendants as prayed for in the petition. This court is now asked to dissolve that injunction, for the reasons set forth in the motions which have been filed, and which, briefly stated, are the following:

"1. That Judge Gilmore, when in another county, and while this court was in session, had no legal authority to grant it.

"2. Because the statements of the petition do not warrant a court of equity in granting the relief asked for, as it is apparent therefrom that he has an adequate remedy at law, and that the grievances complained of, or their continuance, have not and can not work a great or irreparable injury to the plaintiff.

"3. Because the allegations of the petition are untrue.

"To support these a very large number of affidavits have been filed in court here by the defendants, and some (additional to those on which the temporary injunction was allowed) have been produced by the plaintiff, to maintain the allegations of his petition.

"I notice as briefly as I can these grounds in the order named:

"1. Had Judge Gilmore, under the circumstances, the legal right to allow this injunction? I have no doubt whatever as to this question. Section 239 of the code expressly confers the authority to allow injunctions upon the Supreme Court or any judge thereof, the Court of Common Pleas or any judge thereof, or in the absence from the county of said judges, on the Probate Judge of the county where the action is brought.

"There is no limitation in terms that the Judges of the Court of Common Pleas shall be judges of the district in a county of which district the suit is brought, this being settled by the language of the Constitution.

"Nor is there any provision that a judge shall not exercise this power when he is out of the county, when the suit is brought while the court of that county is in session. The only limitation is that imposed by section 246 of the code, which provides that 'no injunction shall be granted by a judge after a motion therefor has been overruled on the merits of the application by his court.' I think, then, that the authority conferred upon a judge of the district to hear such an application under such circumstances is clear and in conformity with the settled opinions and practices of our judges.

"2. Had the plaintiff under the allegations of his petition a right to the relief sought?

"The substance of the allegations of the petition is, that the plaintiff is the lessee of a certain building in the village of Morrow, and is licensed by the government of the United States to and does sell malt and spirituous liquors therein, in accordance with the laws of the State of Ohio, and that he is also licensed to sell tobacco and cigars, and has been carrying on said business there for the past two years according to the laws of Ohio, and strictly in pursuance of said licenses. That his business has been of great profit to him, and would still be so were he not unlawfully disturbed and prevented by defendants from carrying it on.

"He says that on the 26th of January, 1874, the defendants did unlawfully enter in and upon his place of business, and under the pretense of praying, singing, and other devotional exercises, did take possession of said premises for two hours of each and every day, from January 26th until the commencement of the suit, and did prohibit plaintiff's customers, and all other persons who desired to purchase from him the articles kept for sale, from so doing, and have thereby done great injury to the plaintiff. That the defendants unlawfully conspired together to prevent him from carrying on his lawful business, and publicly declared, in the hearing of his customers, that they would never cease invading his premises, blockading his sidewalk, besieging the door of his said place of business, and preventing his customers and all others from entering his premises to purchase the articles kept by him for sale as aforesaid, until his business was wholly destroyed, and that they would compel him to cease his business of selling liquors. And that on the 9th day of February, 1874, the defendants invaded his premises, and prohibited him from practicing his lawful business; and though requested to leave they refused to do so, and occupied the plaintiff's sidewalk and the steps to his door, and prevented all persons from entering his premises and purchasing his articles kept for sale, and declared that they would continue to do so, and heaped epithets upon the plaintiff in the presence of his fellow citizens to disgrace him. Wherefore he prays for an injunction and for damages, which he says he has suffered to the amount of $1,000.

"It is necessary, to a proper decision of the question as to whether the plaintiff has made a case on his petition, to ascertain what the duty of a court of equity is on application to restrain a private nuisance, which, I suppose, is the purpose of this proceeding. What is the law on this subject? Our statutory provisions as to the cases where an injunction should be granted are held to be merely an affirmance of the common law on this point, and the authorities cited from the text books by counsel on each side are valuable as stating under what circumstances this extraordinary remedy should be afforded.

"The law seems to be pretty well settled that equity will interpose to prevent or abate a private nuisance in some cases. That when then it is continuing, permanent, or recurring, an injunction will be granted, unless the injury is such as may be well and adequately compensated in damages; and the loss of health and sleep, the enjoyment of quiet and repose, and the comforts of home, are described as among those which can not be restored or compensated in money; and, using the language of another writer, 'where the loss of health or *trade*, or the destruction of the means of subsistence are affected, an injunction is a proper and appropriate remedy.' And our own Supreme Court, while affirming the doctrine that a court of equity will not, as a general rule, interfere to abate a private nuisance, until the person seeking its aid has established his rights at law, recognize the doctrine that when a nuisance is of such a character as to occasion a personal inconvenience or annoyance, the rule would be different. I am led to the conclusion, then, that a case might be presented to a court of equity, where it would be the duty of a chancellor, on the filing of a petition sustained by proper evidence, to grant an injunction to prevent the exercise of the most solemn acts of worship even, performed with the purest motives, if done under such circumstances, or at such time and place, as to infringe upon the legal rights of others, if they really operated to their substantial injury by the personal annoyance produced and resulting in the loss of trade, and were of a continuing or recurring character. And to apply it to a case like the one at the bar, that if a large number of persons were daily to gather about the place of business of another, who was engaged in a legitimate and proper business (that is, one recognized and allowed by the laws of the State in which we live —for the laws of the land are what courts and citizens alike should respect and maintain), and by singing and prayers, or other means however praiseworthy and commendable under proper circumstances, done against the remonstrance of the person, should so annoy and trouble him as to destroy his peace and comfort, and have the effect to greatly injure or disturb his business, and thus deprive him of the means of subsistence, and it was not merely temporary in its character, but continuing and recurring, I think that not only would they be liable to an action for the recovery of damages done (as I understand to have been admitted by the counsel for the defendants), but that a court of equity would interfere to prevent such infringement upon the rights of others, for these are injuries which can not be adequately compensated by damages, and a plaintiff would not in such a case be driven first to establish his rights at law.

"The question then is, does the plaintiff bring himself within these principles? I do not think he does. In the first place, there is no allegation in his petition—on which alone he can stand—that, except in a single instance, did he ever request this invasion (as he calls it) to cease, or the persons engaged in it to leave his premises. For all that appears from the petition, all the other raids may have been with his full consent; and, indeed, the proof shows such to have been the fact up to the 9th of February, 1874, when for the first and only time, so far as the proof shows, he requested the ladies to desist.

"Nor does his petition allege, either in terms or by implication, that he personally suffered any annoyance, or that irreparable injury to his trade or business had or would accrue. There is no statement that in the aggregate his business has decreased at all, and for all that appears it might have during the period of the holding of the meetings complained of, been better than ever before; and, indeed, there is some evidence of admissions by the plaintiff that such was the fact.

"But there is another ground, which, in my judgment, effectually disposes of this motion. That is the third, viz.: That the allegations of the petition are not true. He alleges that he kept a house where he conducted business according to law. From the nature of the case, the character of this business in this respect is directly in issue, and from the proof it is perfectly clear to my mind that instead of this it was a place where intoxicating liquors were habitually sold, in violation of the laws of the State, and where gambling was constantly being carried on.

"Such a place as this our statute expressly declares to be a public nuisance, and which being shown in a proper case would have to be ordered by the court to be shut up. Now the doctrine is perfectly well settled that a nuisance, either public or private, may be abated even by force, so no breach of the peace is committed. Surely, then, the means used here, with the view of abating this nuisance, were not unlawful or in derogation of the rights of the plaintiff, for as the keeper of such an establishment, the maintainer of a public nuisance, and a gambling house, he can have no standing in a court of equity, when he asks to be protected in his unlawful and criminal business. The injunction will be dissolved at plaintiff's costs."

The people of Morrow were in ecstasy over this legal victory of the women. Scheide, expecting it, had left town. A correspondent, writing of the jubilee on the day the decision was rendered, thus describes the scene:

"As I write the band is playing and marching through our streets, followed by an immense throng of men, women, and children, shouting and rejoicing. Every church bell, school bell, etc., in town is ringing, and two or three locomotives are creating a terrible noise, whistling and ringing their bells. In fact, the entire town is wild with excitement. Hundreds of country people, hearing the noise of the bells and general tumult, are flocking to town from all quarters, many thinking the village was in flames. An immense meeting is now in progress at the Presbyterian church, in addition to the immense throng upon our streets. Speeches are being made, and cheer upon cheer is rending the air. Morrow never had such an awakening, everybody being happy, except the lawyers who defended Scheide, and four or five saloon patrons."

CHAPTER VII.

HOW TO ORGANIZE—THE CONDITIONS OF SUCCESS.

The most active and enthusiastic friends of this great movement are always found to be those who are firmest in the belief that it is of Divine origin, and that no permanent good can be accomplished without implicit reliance upon the Holy Spirit for direction in every stage of the proceedings. The prayerful spirit evinced by the women, and indeed by the whole religious community, wherever the movement has been most successful, can not but challenge the attention of the most skeptical as an evidence that this great reformation is of God and not of man. But God works by the hearts and hands of His servants, and in appointed ways; and it is not difficult for attentive observers of the phenomena of this, as of other great religious revivals, to discern what instruments and modes of procedure He chooses to bless with the most abundant success.

Great care should be exercised by those who inaugurate the movement in a new field, lest its early stages are characterized by some thoughtless act which may bring it before the public in a ridiculous light. "Order is Heaven's first law," and the Divine injunction that all things should be "done decently and in order" is never more applicable than in a movement of this kind. The handful of earnest, but indiscreet women who, excited by the stories of conquest in the West, started out in the streets of Philadelphia without preparatory meetings or proper organization, only to be hooted at by rowdies, insulted by saloon-keepers, and derided by the skeptical press, have only themselves to thank that their zeal and self-sacrifice was productive of no good result. That the Ohio movement has not yet been successful in the East is not because it is not as well adapted to Eastern as to Western civilization, as many are disposed to think, but simply to the fact that it has never been fairly tried.

The suggestions which follow are from the pen of Dr. Dio Lewis, whose ideas are entitled to weight, not only because of his connection with the movement when it was yet in its incipient form, but because of his remarkable success as an organizer. They are the result of careful study and reflection after his return from his second visit to Ohio (in February), where he observed the movement from various standpoints. They were prepared especially for this work:

HINTS AS TO PLAN OF ORGANIZATION—BY DIO LEWIS.

"1. Assuming that the women are deeply interested, and have met in earnest union prayer meetings, I think the following steps constitute the best course:

"A general meeting of citizens is called. The largest place in town is crowded. A chairman and secretary are chosen, a prayer, and a song by all, and now the clergymen and other prominent citizens are called upon to make *two-minute* speeches.

"A committee of five—three women and two men—is next chosen to come forward, and, sitting where they can look into the faces of the audience, select an executive committee, exclusively of women, one from each church, and from the large churches two or three. The Catholic Church should be well represented, and outside of the churches there may be good active women who should have a place on the committee.

"2. A committee of men, consisting of one from each church,

and two or three from the largest churches, and two or three well-known citizens outside the churches, and one man to represent the Sons of Temperance, one the Good Templars, and one from each of the other organizations, as the Masons and Odd Fellows, one to represent the insurance companies, one the lawyers, one the doctors, and one the merchants. These gentlemen constitute the Advisory Business Committee.

"3. After additional speeches, songs, and prayers the meeting adjourns to meet at ten o'clock the next morning to complete the organization.

"4. At the morning meeting the various members of the two committees chosen the evening before will give the names of the most earnest women in the several organizations they were chosen to represent, which names have been prepared by special suggestion at the previous meeting. The number of new names thus presented to the morning meeting, including the Executive Committee, should be equal to one hundred women for every twenty-five dram-shops in the town. These women constitute the committees to visit saloons.

"5. At this morning meeting a committee of five or ten women is appointed to visit all places of business in town and request the proprietors to close from ten to eleven every morning, to give all who are thus disposed to assemble in the churches to hold what is called the business men's prayer meetings. As each business house will secure its own proper share of the business, no objection is generally made to the closing. The dram-shops are now the only places open. With all the others shut, the bells tolling the whole hour, and many men assembled in the churches for prayer, while the women are marching on the saloons, constitutes altogether a good and wise management.

"6. It is well for the Saloon Committees to count about fifty each, a certain portion of the town being set off to each committee.

"7. A visiting committee halts at a saloon, and the leader asks permission to enter. If this is granted, when they are all inside, an appeal from the women to the dealer in intoxicating drinks is read, followed by singing and prayer. It is wise to begin or end the prayer with the Lord's Prayer, in which all can join.

"The women generally remain from ten to thirty minutes. If

they are not admitted, these exercises are held on the sidewalk or in the street."

There is little to add to these suggestions except that the women alone should do all the street work, but that the men, and especially the business men of the community, should neglect no opportunity to manifest by peaceful methods their sympathy with the women and their intention to stand by them through good and through evil report. The ministers should be outspoken in their sympathy on proper occasions, and let it be understood that as this is a religious work it has their best wishes. Nothing strengthens the women or alarms the saloon-keepers more than the knowledge that public sentiment—the sentiment of the good people of all denominations and parties—is in favor of this mode of closing dram-shops.

"Peace, prayer, and persuasion," is a brief alliterative statement of the only means to be employed in this movement; but a fuller and more satisfactory expression of the creed of the crusaders is to be found in the admirable resolutions adopted by the Ohio State Convention, or the Women's Temperance Association, and published in another chapter of this book. If the principles there laid down are consistently and persistently adhered to success seems almost unavoidable.

CHAPTER VIII.

THE MOVEMENT BECOMES NATIONAL.

LONG before the State Convention of the Women's Temperance Association the movement had proved such a decided success in Ohio that friends of the cause in other States organized in a similar manner and entered upon the work. Shelbyville, Indiana, was moved upon as early as January 20th; but the ladies have met with only limited success. At Jeffersonville, in that State, some very disgraceful acts have been perpetrated on the part of the saloonatics, which led us to conclude that the State's Prison is very appropriately located there. At Richmond the movement has begun with better auspices and promise of complete success. At Indianapolis the ladies have so far devoted most of their energies to defeating applications for license and stirring up the men to execute the Baxter law against liquor-selling, in both of which they have been very successful. The movement is also in progress at Hartford City, Blufftown, Muncie, North Vernon, Winchester, and other points in Indiana; and in spite of repeated discouragements great good has been accomplished.

In Chicago the movement was started in a rather irregular manner, and abandoned without anything being accomplished. In San Francisco, California, the ladies are perfecting their organization, but have not taken the field yet. In Omaha and Lincoln, Nebraska, the work has been entered upon with vigor, but reports of success are as yet rather meager. The movement nowhere seems to meet with that complete success

THE MOVEMENT BECOMES NATIONAL. 83

achieved in Ohio and Eastern Indiana. In New York City, and Philadelphia, the Temperance Alliance is organizing carefully, intending to exhaust all other means before entering upon a system of visitation and prayer. In some of the larger cities the attempt to suppress the saloons on the Ohio plan of operations against them, has been abandoned; and it will be even a larger undertaking in Cincinnati where there is an immense German population, and very few among them who regard the manufacture and consumption of malt liquors and wines as either sinful, immoral, or harmful. Educated from their youth up to drink beer and wine with as much freedom as water, and very rarely indulging in either to excess, they regard any attempt to deprive them of these beverages as an encroachment upon private rights which they will resist to the bitter end. The opposition encountered by the praying women in the German quarter of Columbus is but a feeble foreshadowing of what will happen when the organizing bands take up their line of march across the Rhine.

In Massachusetts the movement can not yet be said to be well organized. Dr. Lewis insists that the system is just as practicable there as here; but there seems to be an invincible repugnance in the New England (especially the Bostonian) mind to adopting anything which had its origin in the West or South. The following from the Springfield (Mass.) *Republican* will give a clear idea of the New England ideas upon the subject, the peculiar difficulties in their way, and the plan upon which they have decided:

"THE WORCESTER WOMEN'S WAR ON WHISKY.

"Decidedly the most interesting, not to say important, event of the week to the Massachusetts people has been the problem the women of Worcester have been working out, scarcely less for their sex throughout New England than for themselves. Ever since the interest excited by the novel campaign of the Ohio women against intemperance was increased by the announcement that Dio Lewis proposed to try the same tactics in the central city of Massachusetts, curiosity and speculation have been growing as to the probable result. People who appreciated the radical difference between the conditions under which the Western movement had its birth, and those of a New England community, felt pretty sure that it could not survive the transplantment. At the same time, there had been such peculiar, even wonderful, features connected with the Ohio campaign, that it seemed possible it might prove one of those phenomena which occasionally set at defiance all social and natural laws, and that the conservative East might be destined to repeat the experience of the unconventional West.

"Such was the state of the public mind when Lewis appeared on the stage Monday evening. Before he had closed his speech it was plain enough that he had in his audience several hundred women who were ready for vigorous work—something that promised to be more telling than going to temperance conventions and sitting by while the men declaimed the conventional speeches against the 'demon of intemperance,' and resolved that something ought to be done to arrest his progress. Not a few seemed so much impressed by the earnestness and enthusiasm of the apostle of the Ohio movement as to be almost ready for his plan of starting out for the saloons before sunset the next day. The large majority, however, had a more correct appreciation of the difficulties which they must encounter than their decidedly illogical orator, and the extent of these difficulties grew upon them the more they talked the matter over among themselves. Lewis wanted them to pray in the saloons till the keepers would close up, but—as is the case in most Massachusetts towns under the con, stabulary *regime*—only a few of the half-thousand drinking places in the city are saloons, or even, publicly, places for selling liquor, a great many of them being known to few but the police, and known to them not by any sign of bars, but by the drunkards who issue from them. To attempt the ferreting out of all these places was seen to be plainly a hopeless task, and to stop in such a work before success was reached would be immeasurably worse than if nothing had been attempted. So the Worcester women soon decided not to essay such a Quixotical proceeding.

"Having decided what not to do, the even more important question remained—what system they should adopt, for they were plainly in earnest to do something. Even Lewis himself, though he saw them rejecting his counsels, was deeply impressed with their earnestness, and we hear of his saying that nowhere in Ohio has he seen anything that equaled it. Nothing was more strongly marked than the determination to turn this earnestness into some practical channel. The plan they have settled upon is already familiar to our readers—one of private, personal appeal, not only to the liquor-seller, but to his, in so many instances, equally guilty partner—the property holder, who rents him his shop. Instead of marching through the streets and attempting to pray down the obnoxious liquor-seller, till he should yield an unwilling, and probably only temporary, surrender to escape their presence, the Worcester women propose to labor with him quietly, two or three at a time, and try by private entreaty and prayer to persuade him to give up the business. At the same time, and in the same way, the the owner of the shop is to be urged to sign a pledge not to let any of his property for liquor-selling. Hotel keepers and druggists are also to be visited in a similar way, and the proceedings being in the most marked contrast with the Ohio way of doing things.

"This may be fairly considered as the settlement of the question for New England, quite as much as for Worcester. We scarcely need to say that we consider such an adaptation of the Western system immeasurably wiser than an attempt to transfer it bodily into a climate so uncongenial. Both are equally signs of a deep and genuine temperance revival, which seems destined to affect, in greater or less degree, the whole country. Both are manifestations of a reviving belief in the quite generally discarded 'moral suasion' movement against intemperance, and as such the most encouraging signs the reform has seen since the Washingtonian movement of a generation ago."

Meanwhile the movement continues to spread, and with astonishing success, in Central and Southern Ohio.

Every day brings account of beginnings at places hitherto thought hopeless; and every night we are surprised and gladdened by telegrams from two or three towns that "all the bells are ringing—bonfires in the streets—bands playing—everybody happy—the last saloon has surrendered." Every day the enemies of the movement make fresh prophecies, and each succeeding day sees them falsified.

About ninety towns and cities are now either in the thick of the contest, entering upon it, or resting after victory. At London, Madison county, six saloons and three drug stores have been closed, and twelve hundred people have signed the pledge. I visited London soon after the inception of the movement, and Mrs. B. F. Custer, Secretary of the Association, gave me an account which is considered a fair representation of the feeling: "We want you to particularly understand that this is not a mere temporary excitement, the result of womanly impulse. We do not expect to stop the traffic immediately, but have set in for months, it may be years, of hard work. We have labored harder to keep down excitement than to create it. I, for one, will not be identified with any mere wave of enthusiasm. It is folly for us to expect that when we have wickedly and willfully allowed a vast evil to grow up among us, God will suddenly relieve us of it and abolish it. He will not take away our free agency in any such way. I am pained to hear some ladies say they have staked their Christian faith on the success of this movement. Such a prayer-test as that would be nothing less than mockery. We intend to work on, pray on, sing on, and talk on till we get the public opinion up to the point of sustaining the law, and then there will still be plenty to do."

THE MOVEMENT BECOMES NATIONAL. 87

Among the other prominent workers are Mrs. Dr. Sharp, Mrs. T. Custer, President; Mrs. Duncan and Mrs. Toland Vice-Presidents, and Miss Laura Kinney, Reader. They have selections of Scripture read, with the prayers and singing. Rev. C. W. Finley, Presbyterian, Rev. T. H. Munroe, Methodist, and Mr. Glover, Universalist, are the only Protestant ministers engaged. The Catholics have taken a very active part, however, and the movement has the sanction of the priest.

At Athens the work was prosecuted with unusual vigor, and in one month eight saloons and three drug stores were closed. (Perhaps "pledged" would be more appropriate for the drug stores.) Only two saloons remain open. But they might as well surrender with a good grace, for public opinion is up to the "high moral" point, and the law will finish what the Gospel does not.

At Zaleski a complete victory was gained in two weeks. All the saloons are closed, all the drug-stores "pledged," and nearly the whole adult population have signed the pledge. At Jamestown every saloon is closed. At Waynesville and Corwin (on opposite sides of the Little Miami) every saloon is closed. Thomas Franey, "the most gentlemanly saloonatic in Ohio," held out a long time, but he was too much of a gentleman for such a business, and yielded just in time to save his credit. At Reeseville the ladies carried things as by storm; three saloons were closed almost before the saloonatics knew what hurt them. Logan, in the Hocking Valley, looked to me like Morrow—a hopeless case. In a population of 2,500 it had twenty-three saloons. The saloonatics were all men of property, worth everywhere from twenty to a hundred thousand dollars each.

The place is surrounded by mining towns (coal), and its Saturday nights were often made hideous by drunken miners. The ladies entered upon their work the first of February; the first of March only one saloon remained! McArthur, Vinton county, was cleared of the liquor traffic in six weeks. At Chillicothe the movement proceeds slowly, but we are assured with certainty of final success.

Time and space fail me to set forth the various places redeemed and the good accomplished. These figures do not represent the most important features of the progress. Its educational effects, both morally and intellectually, have been immense. It has waked the people up to their duty. The women have discovered their immense moral power against intemperance, and they will use it. Their social power on the subject is yet to be tested; but I, for one, believe it to be much greater than the means now employed. If every matron would close her parlor to, and every maiden decline all attentions from, any young man who habitually used intoxicating liquors, there would be a greater reform than could be effected by forty Adair laws or Baxter bills. But this is hardly a just comparison, for a reform need not be very great to exceed that effected by those laws.

This movement has also educated the popular intellect. It has set men to earnest thinking who had not been in the habit; it put men to committee work, and in other places, where their latent faculties were developed. The genius of the movement has been: Put every man and woman where he or she will do the most good, whether at talking, writing, singing, committee work or leading in religious exercises. Above all it has worked men up to the importance of enforcing what laws we have on the subject I am not, myself, an enthusiast for general prohibitory laws, but I think the wisdom of our legislators might give us a general ordinance which would enable the people of any one town or district to forbid the establishment of saloons without being governed by their neighbors. Local self-government, with the women's movement to help, would clear two-thirds of the small towns of whisky-shops. It would not stop all whisky drinking, of course; it will take some generations to do that. But it would remove those standing temptations which are continually creating a new army of drunkards.

But are there no evils connected with this movement? Verily, there are, and some serious ones, too. When it began prophecies were abundant as to the evils that would result. Particularly it was expected that as it spread it would gradually grow less effective; that saloon-keepers would devise new methods of resistance, and when the novelty wore off men would sell and drink regardless of the presence of women. This has proved only partially true. New defenses have been overcome by new methods of attack; the movement appears to gather strength rather than lose, and where the fair crusaders have been careful to keep within the law, their power has suffered no diminution.

One evil to be feared more than all others was the natural tendency of all such movements to run into fanaticism, and be controlled by mere blind impulse. But I am surprised to see how successfully this evil has been avoided in most instances. There is no other feature in which the ladies have shown such admirable tact and judgment as in guiding the popular enthusiasm; and the methods by which they have controlled it deserve notice. Whenever a man got obstreperous they would sing him into calm reason. At many an evening meeting I have attended I have seen some muscular Christian, or fighting Methodist, get terribly excited over the liquor traffic, or some slight he thought the ladies had received, and talk in a way that, if let alone, would excite a mob spirit But the ladies would at once strike up, "Come ye that love the Lord," or "There is a fountain filled with blood," or some more subduing strain, and even as David's harp charmed the evil spirit out of Saul, the song brought down the warlike mind to a calm temper. When a man got unusually angry, some venerable lady or old Christian brother would deliver a fervent prayer for humility and a contrite heart, and all would be well again.

But I have noticed one evil occasionally, the relation of which may wound the feelings of the devout. In many instances this movement has caused a profanation of prayer. People of peculiar organizations, who are not careful to distinguish between their own impulses and the "promptings of the Spirit," have been led to utter extravagances, which would grate harshly on the ear at any time, but are positively shocking in a prayer. If I may so express it, they did not pray to God so much as at the saloon-keeper, imagining that zeal for the cause and anger at its opponents were equally the results of Divine promptings; their prayers were not petitions to the Creator so much as threats of Divine vengeance on the rum-sellers and passionate appeals to the hearers. Some such evil as this, so natural to poor humanity, seems inseparable from all popular excitements, in which the religious emotions play an active part. "The great army of the queer and crazy," as aptly described by Mary Clemmer Ames, seem instinctively attracted to such movements; and, as if it were planned by the devil himself, they so mix up with the movement that they appear to the world as its accredited leaders.

Luther did not have half the trouble with pope and priest that he did with those wild reformers who maintained that "Christian liberty" meant liberty to follow the patriarchs into polygamy and concubinage, and to be independent of earthly rulers and magistrates. And I imagine the women suffragists of to-day would rather have ten thousand Todds, Bushnells, and Hollands against them than *one* Woodhull with them. That something of that nature attends on this is not to be wondered at; but I can safely say that I never witnessed a movement that had so little. That the ladies have so managed as to almost avoid that entanglement, I consider their greatest triumph. The legal difficulty in the way is not so easily settled. Christianity is not incorporated in the law of Ohio, and I have no more right, under the Constitution, to sing and pray before a man's door against his will than he has to whistle and dance before mine. I observe that one judge goes farther, and says that public prayer for a man against his will, no matter where, is an infringement of private right. "His name is his private property, and must not be used in such a way as to bring him into unpleasant notoriety or public contempt." It will certainly be a novelty in jurisprudence if men take out an injunction to prevent women praying for them. But I suspect there are very few dealers who will appeal to the law. Those who are without the law must be judged accordingly, and if there is one saloon-keeper in ten in this country who keeps within the law, I haven't the evidence to convince me of it. I remember, however, an injunction case of a similar nature, that is reported in Second Kings, and that was dissolved rather suddenly by a higher Court.

Take it in any light we will, this movement is worthy of attention. Even in the lowest political view it is important, for more than one local election, and probably some general elections, will turn upon it. To the higher class of statesmen, who recognize the fact that all parties embodying great principles must be built up by slow and separately insensible increments, it is of interest as an important factor in the work. The attention of the philosopher is called to it as a unique phenomenon, and the sociologists might see in it an important point in the progress of social evolution. The Christian, of course, will see in it a remarkable illustration of the power of prayer and moral force. And whether right or wrong, the Christian has this advantage: his view includes all that is good in all the others, and has a special element of personal comfort besides.

The indirect effects of the Women's War on Whisky are deserving of notice. It is generally true that when any great movement like this sweeps over the country, enlisting tens of thousands in the cause, every man with an *ism* starts up and tries to hitch the movement on to his car. The advocates of prohibitory liquor laws, of woman suffrage, and of the religious amendment " God-in-the-Constitution "—severally-see in this movement a heaven-sent proof of the goodness of their cause and an aid to its success. At first it seemed that this work would be a wonderful help to woman-suffrage; but later developments show rather the contrary. In the first place the leading women who advocate suffrage for their sex have taken strong ground against this movement. Besides the pronunciamentos from Mrs. Cady Stanton, and others, the following letter from Mrs. Swisshelm shows the animus of that class:

" *To the Editor of the New York Tribune:*

"SIR: The daily press has been largely occupied of late with details of the war which women have waged with the liquor traffic in some of our Western States; and, so far as I have observed, its sentiment seems to be generally in favor of the attack, while the defense has small share of sympathy. As the question thus raised lies deeper than a few illegal prayer meetings in the snow, will you allow me a little space for its consideration?

"In her address before the Judiciary Committee of the House of Representatives, in Washington, against the right of any woman to take any part in political affairs, Mrs. Guthrie said, that 'man is, by nature and by God, the keeper and guardian of women and children.' That this is physically true, there is no room for doubt. No man can honestly live to himself. The gifts of one are the inheritance of all. The strong, by the gift of strength, is made the helper of the weak; the wise, by his wisdom, the teacher of the foolish; the pure, by his purity, the guide of the impure—and so on to the end. Our best belongs to the world; our worst is our own. Bacon's wisdom and greatness were important items in the schedule of the world's wealth. His meanness alone was his private property. Man's superior muscle makes him the muscular guardian of women and children, and lays upon him onerous duties, which he seldom shirks. Even savage men make their bodies a wall of defense for the women of their tribe, and that man lacks manhood whose instinct does not prompt him to spring between a woman or child and physical harm. This instinct is something different from that which makes the strong man the guardian of the infirm of his own sex, and lies deep in the Creator's plan for the perpetuation of the race.

"To one who thinks calmly, and recognizes man's natural guardianship of woman, it is wonderful to see hundreds of thousands of able-bodied men stand aside and cheer a few thousand feeble women on to such a wasting, hopeless, physical contest. What is it all but a trial of physical strength between the liquor dealers and their assailants, with all the conditions in favor of the former? Who does not know it is hopeless? Who does not know that the man can sit longer by his hot stove than the women can kneel in the snow? Who does not know that he must win the case when it comes before the courts? Who does not know that the law is on his side? Who does not know that they have no more right to encumber a sidewalk with a prayer-meeting tent than with a pig pen? Who does not know that they have no more right to go into a man's house without his consent, or to hinder his lawful business by crowding his doorstep, than he has to set up a bar in the parlor of any one of them? Who does not know that these women are reënacting the part of the old sheep who knocked his own brains out butting a swinging mallet? The thing seems at every stroke to give way, but returns with rebound to strike the striker, while the men who encourage the onslaught are like the boy who hung up the mallet.

"With a word, a turn of the hand, men made the laws which they prompt women to violate. Without physical labor, by the exercise of a great moral power, they intrench the rum traffic in its present position; then, as a 'sop to Cerberus,' quiet their consciences by throwing up their hats for the women who attack those intrenchments, by pitting their powers of physical endurance against those of the garrison. The implement which raised the fortifications is the ballot; and this is the only power competent to overthrow them. If it is not right for woman to wield this power, it is not wise for her to contend against it, with only physical endurance as a weapon. It is, in fact, a complete reversal of the natural position of the sexes; for, as physical force is man's sphere, so is moral power woman's; and in as far as he exceeds her in muscle does she excel him in moral perception. To deny her the use of that most efficient moral weapon, a vote, and then urge her into a physical contest with it, is very like saying that women can not use artillery or Spencer rifles, but ought to form the advance in an attack upon an army well drilled in their use, and sending them forward armed with broadswords, shields, javelins, and other implements of mediæval warfare. This is certainly poor generalship, and suggests the idea of surplus troops, which it would be more economical to bury than provision. Soldiers who can not be intrusted with weapons of equal power with those of the enemy, should be mustered out, and never should have been mustered in.

"Men alone have assumed the responsibility of government. Let them bear it alone or acknowledge they can not. If they feel that they have been legislating themselves into drunkards' graves, and can not do otherwise, let them look for the cause; and if they find that the Creator was right when he said, 'It is not good for man to be alone,' and gave to man and woman a joint dominion over the earth, let them call on their natural, heaven-appointed allies; let them restore to them their equal dominion, which men have feloniously taken away, and say, 'help us and yourselves; join with us in preserving our children from the rum fiend! Help us to save the world! We will bear the brunt in physical war, you on the moral battle-field. United we stand, divided we fall! Together we can face and conquer all the powers of darkness! Come with us, not as our property, but as our partners, in time and in eternity, in joy and in sorrow, in conflict and in victory!' When they are ready to do this they will find women, even Mrs. Guthrie, ready to respond; but until they are, let them do their own fighting with the creature of their own creation, and the carnal weapons of physical force which of right belong to them.

"JANE GREY SWISSHELM.
"CHICAGO, ILL., February 12, 1874."

It seems to be the idea of such women that if men would only make "good laws," every thing would be lovely. And no doubt, when those women enter our legislatures we shall have plenty of "moral reform" laws. With what result every experienced man can easily predict; for, among all the uncertainties of law and society, one thing is everlastingly certain: The unexpected and indirect results of any law are always greater than the direct and expected.

But while a few have been converted, many more have been convinced by this movement that in moral matters women can do far more than voters. In politics women could only do what we have done—pass temperance laws and elect men to execute them. A quarter of a century's experience has shown the futility of that. Our laws are too good now. The average moral sentiment of the laws is above the average moral sense of the people. Such laws are due to the special efforts of exceptionally good men, who labor to get them on the statute-book, and then are vastly surprised to find that laws do not execute themselves. The advocates of this reform assume that a state of society could exist in which the women were so far independent of the men that they could adopt a scheme of civil polity in opposition to the wish of a majority of the men, or having adopted, enforce it. And this when the census of Ohio shows that, with the exception of one in twelve, every woman of voting age is the intimate bosom friend, business partner, and trusted counselor of some man; that four-fifths of the property is in the hands of men, and nine-tenths of the ability to earn more, and that men won't enforce their own laws if they don't like them, much less those of women. The proposition is briefly this: Men are to hand over half their political power to women, that women may turn around and use that power to compel men to do right. The genius who lifted himself over the stile by his boot-straps must have been the inventor of this scheme. I should naturally hesitate to hand a woman a club if she had previously declared her intention to "swat me over the head" with it. And it seems to me that what men are unwilling to do, they will hardly give women the power to compel them to do.

And while it is doubtful whether many friends of temperance have been gained, it is certain that all the enemies of this movement are made the enemies of women suffrage. There is in this country a growing dread of the influence of the church, *as such*, in politics; and many undoubted friends of temperance have grave fears that they will, by alliance with this movement, be dragged into other schemes for which they have no sympathy. Such regard women suffrage as only an aid to "God-in-the-Constitution," and a union of Church and State.

The prohibitionists have been scarcely more fortunate in capturing this movement. Whether this result was due to the position of Dr. Lewis or not, we can hardly say; but whenever called upon to give his views, he has opposed prohibitory legislation. At Dayton he gave his views at length. He gave a full history of such legislation in Massachusetts. He had once favored it, and labored for it, but he now saw his mistake. It had injured the cause by leading men to trust in law. The Washingtonians had been laboring to save drunkards by love and kindness, but when the law came they put their hands in their pockets and said, "Now let her work," and she would not work. They had the most law-abiding people in the world, and a prohibitory law so good that the devil himself could not pick a flaw in it. Yet they had thirty-five hundred rum-holes in Boston, and more drunkenness than before in the State. He felt impelled to thus talk because this women's work met with so much hindrance from men who put their trust in law. Our experience of a quarter of a century in Indiana seems to teach the same lesson.

The reasons for this imperfect operation of prohibitory laws are not far to seek. And even in those cases where such laws appear to be doing great good, it is well to inquire if their operation is not creating among the people habits of thought which will eventually work out far greater evils than any the laws can remove. It can not be doubted that our popular institutions have their root deep in the democratic idea that it is nobody's business what a man does to his own hurt; and that the liquor traffic only comes within the province of the legislature in so far as it enables a man to maintain a nuisance against the wish of the community. Upon this principle the "local option" feature of our law appeared to me correct, enabling each community to decide for itself whether it would sustain the sale of liquor. But I suspect the great error of the temperance men has consisted in going beyond this, and maintaining the right of the State to regulate individual conduct wherever it seemed good to the majority to do so.

Two theories of civil government were presented for our forefathers' consideration: the paternal, assuming that it is the business of government to "take care of the people," and permit them to do only that which is for their good; and the opposite doctrine, that it is the province of government to leave each man as much as possible to himself, and only interfere with him when he interferes with some other man's personal freedom or property. No matter which was the true theory originally, there can be no question that the Constitutional Fathers adopted the latter; that they intended a cheap and simple form of government, which should not touch the individuality of the citizen at one point in a thousand of his daily life. But, unfortunately, habits of political thought endure long after the facts which gave rise to them have passed away; and the old European idea of a paternal, religious, or moral reform government still lingers in the minds of a large class of our people. "Why don't the government do something?" is a question I have heard at least a hundred times since the late panic; and to the minds of such people the two facts that a certain thing is an evil, and we should be better off if it were abolished, are ample reasons for governmental interference. "Something must be done—government ought to take hold and do it. Whatever government undertakes, if the law is sufficiently stringent, will be accomplished." Such is virtually their logic—though they do not put it so definitely.

And this seems to me the great evil of all prohibitory liquor laws; they familiarize the minds of the people with the daily interference of government in their private affairs. They raise up a hateful brood of spies and informers. They send men spying into our back kitchens or private closets, to see what we drink; and then to following our steps to see where we buy it. Honorable men instinctively shrink from this sort of business, and no matter how fairly the reformers start out, you will notice that the actual business of filing information or making affidavits soon slides down into the hands of men whom we do not readily take to. This honorable reluctance to "turn informer" on one's neighbor, to have him fined for an "ordinary drink," is not without its resulting embarrassment; but can we afford to have it abolished? Suppose we could create such a furore for temperance that men would generally give notice of their neighbors' sale, purchase, or use of liquor—yea, suppose we could thereby abolish the traffic altogether—and to that complexion must it come if we abolish it by law—though at the cost of breaking down this instinctive reluctance, would not our loss far outweigh our gain? The moralist comes to me and says: "Sir, it is bad for you to drink." The prohibitionist says: "Sir, you shall not drink; and if you do, we'll put you in jail or make you tell where you got your liquor!" And all the natural man and democratic American in me fires up to reply, "I'll drink what I please." And if the law does imprison me for refusing to tell where I obtained my liquor, the community has an instinctive feeling that personal liberty has been outraged, and one or two such cases render the enforcement of the law in that community impossible. The moral suasionist presents himself as a friend, the law as an enemy. The chances are a hundred to one that the toper will listen to the first where he would resist the second.

Another serious defect in the prohibitory law is, that it is only effective as to the poor, but a dead letter as to the rich. And any law of which that is true is certain to be a failure in this democratic country. The retail shop, where the poor man gets his drink, can be shut up, but the wealthy use as much liquor as ever. At least a hundred fines have been inflicted for drunkenness in one town within the year—every one of them upon poor laboring men—while I have known a score of "drunks" among the wealthy and socially powerful without even a threat of arrest. It is scarcely necessary to quote here the homely proverb, "What is everybody's business is nobody's business," but it is evident that a law which does not specifically call upon some one person or set of persons for enforcement contains within itself the elements of defeat. It is easy enough to say, "The law is good enough, if people would only enforce it." Similarly, if the stone you throw up would stay in the air, it would not fall and break anybody's head. But there is a law of nature operating by reason of which the stone will not stay in the air; and there is a law none the less real, though more subtle, by which statutes aimed at merely personal vices will either be irregularly enforced or totally disregarded. When a man is murdered, his friends—or the man himself and his friends, if his property be taken or his person harmed—are all alive to the importance of justice; every eye is open, every ear turned to catch the slightest whisper which may lead to the arrest of the offender. And, when arrested, the prosecuting witness is the natural ally of the law; no threats of the court are required to make him testify, and thus it is two against one—State and witness against the offender. But in case of personal vices, particularly drunkenness, the offender and the one on whom the act is done are in collusion against the law; their interests are to defeat the prosecutor, and the unwilling witness either evades the court entirely, or withholds the most important evidence. It is here again two against one, but the one is the law. Hence, laws against murder, theft, and the like, have an inherent tendency toward enforcement, no matter how loosely or awkwardly worded; but laws against personal vices naturally tend to fall into disuse; and thus a prohibitory liquor law must be far more stringent and clearly worded than ordinary criminal law; and to render it effective, the powers of government must be increased ten fold.

The State of Indiana can enforce her Criminal Code with tolerable certainty; but to enforce the Baxter bill, it will be necessary not only to vastly strengthen the prerogatives of each local official, but create a *censor morum*, whose specific duty it shall be to file information against offenders, upon which the justice can issue warrants. The advocate of temperance laws too often lose sight of the distinction between sin and crime. The latter will be punished on the evidence of the injured party; punishment of the former must depend on society at large, unless the government name a censor, as suggested. But the experience of all constitutional governments has shown that an increase or extension of the powers of government always results in one of two evils—either each separate arm of government grows weaker in proportion as the arms are extended, or in the desperate attempt to strengthen them the central power grows too great for the liberty of the citizen; and thus government on the one hand degenerates into anarchy, or on the other strengthens into despotism. The former tendency is now apparent in our laws—at least one-fifth of them are practically void. One-fifth of our statutes might be repealed to-morrow, and the observer would note no difference in the ordinary workings of society. The prohibitionists must now address to their consciences this question: Is the suppression of the liquor traffic of such transcendent importance that we should, to compass it, grant extraordinary powers to government: and if we do grant these powers, will the evil stop there?

Another serious difficulty with such a law is the ease with which it can be made an instrument of private revenge. In this it is like our Sunday law, "provoke" law, "profanity" law, and a dozen others referred to above. Nobody ever thinks of enforcing them in a general way; but occasionally some mean-spirited soul, who has conceived a spite against his neighbor, lies in wait till he hears him swear, or sees him violate some other one of our many "dead-letter laws," then hies him to a justice and takes his mean revenge by means of the law. Of course the injured party, seeing that the statute is only revived at rare instances for an unworthy purpose, looks upon the government as an enemy rather than a friend, and he and his become enemies of the law. Several such cases have already occurred under our temperance law. Disregard for such statutes insensibly teaches men contempt for all law, and the measure of legal power becomes the measure of right.

For twenty years it has been "orthodox" to favor prohibitory laws, to see only the reasons in their favor, and ignore the difficulties. On men who took no active part in the reform the effect of such a one-sided system was bad enough; but on those who made it a hobby much worse. In zeal for this one reform they lost sight of collateral issues; though constant failure attended the law they refused to return to the moral and educational methods by which a partial success had been secured, and insisted on "more stringent measures." Ignoring the evils almost certain to result from such laws, the radical temperance men too often appear as a set of impracticables. To many of them it was nothing that such legislation trenched on individual liberty, that it raised a brood of spies and informers; that it cultivated hypocrisy, perjury, and evasion of law; that it familiarized the popular mind with a coerced morality, and gave rise to more dangers and evils than it cured. Their action might have been appropriate, and their plan practical, under a different political system; but under ours, I can not but conclude that all such repressive systems will fail. The ideas of those who favor such legislation appear to me only a "survival" of those which prevailed under the older "paternal governments." Once they were useful, and their action assisted to make the present condition possible; now they are a hindrance, leading men to trust that to written law, which can only be accomplished by moral and educational methods. We are in a transition state, and our laws are a compromise between the past and the future, answering, though somewhat awkwardly, the needs of the present. Nominally, and in the written constitution, "paternal government" is abrogated; practically, and in the minds of many of the people, we retain the standards of political thought and governmental creeds of the old system. That we are so able to develop the new, while the old still clings to us, is one of the hopeful signs of the times. Constant experiments on the old plan, under the new conditions, followed in course by constant failure, will finally teach the most impracticable that new wine can not safely be put in old bottles; that a system eminently practicable under a monarch with a standing army, is eminently absurd where the people must enforce the law upon themselves; that a popular government can not make people good by law; but that virtue, temperance, and general morality must depend on individual action and moral suasion, the only benefit of law being to prevent undue interference with the good by the violent and bad.

The Women's War has elicited a thousand or more songs, poems, and hymns. From a half-bushel or so offered I select, as a fitting finale to this somewhat lengthy digression on prohibition and other reforms, the best one—written by a gentleman who believes in all the *isms* from "God-in-the-Constitution" down. While the composition is not above criticism, the meter not quite faultless, and the measure not exactly

Spenserian, yet the life and spirit are good; and while I dissent from all the author's conclusions I agree measurably with his premises.

THE WOMAN'S PROBLEM.

BY GEORGE KATES.

'The sounds of war come from afar
    With victory songs to cheer us,
While sacred airs and fervent prayers
    Ascend from voices near us.

It is a cry ascending high
    From stricken hearts, all bleeding,
Whose prayer and song recite a wrong
    All other wrongs exceeding—

A giant wrong, alert and strong,
    Entrenched in human weakness,
Before whose shrines, 'mid glowing wines,
    The brave bow down in meekness.

Love fades and dies in bloated eyes;
    The strong their strength surrender;
While manhood falls prostrate, and crawls
    Before the arch offender.

While millions feel his iron heel
    And writhe beneath its power,
They seek in vain redress to gain
    From men who serve the hour.

For those we send our laws to mend
    Consult their purse and palates,
Till every law presents a flaw
    To serve their master's valets.

When helpless man beneath this ban
    Let fall his hands despairing,
'Twas women's hour to try her power,
    In deeds of love and daring.

THE WOMEN'S WAR ON WHISKY.

Calm and alert, with faith begirt,
   Of malice all defiant;
With gentle hand she grasps her wand,
   And wrestles with the giant!

Ye gods and men, with golden pen,
   Write down her deeds of valor!
Write on the page: "'Tis woman's age;
   And demons quail in pallor."

Breathless we stand, and watch her wand,
   That waves in conflict yonder;
While song and prayer fill all the air
   With problems men may ponder.

As goes the fight 'twixt wrong and right,
   Her wand still waving higher,
The demon moans in bitter tones
   'Neath love's resistless fire.

Shall you and I stand idly by,
   Without a voice to cheer her,
While hell sends up its battle cry
   From tongues that vilely jeer her?

Shall we, whose hearts should be our charts
   Stand croaking like the raven,
While her fair hand waves high the wand
   That points us to a haven?

Are we not men with mother ken;
   In this republic sovereign?
With vote and voice to make a choice
   Of how, and who shall govern?

"Ah! yes," say you, "but still, 'tis true
   We lack the force of numbers,"
Then let us rise and ope our eyes,
   From out our listless slumbers!

And talk no more, as wont of yore,
    Of arms and hearts of yeomen;
The way is plain, the right to gain—
    Enfranchise glorious women!

At least, we'll pray: God speed the day
    When victory's wreath shall crown her;
And every State, from small to great,
    Shall in the franchise own her!

While now she kneels where manhood reels,
    Amid his foul pollution,
Then both shall stand with hand in hand—
    This problem's grand solution.

Where now she stoops, 'mid vulgar groups,
    To raise her fallen brother,
She'll stand erect with those elect,
    Who council each with other.

In her franchise full power lies
    To offer firm resistance
To venal rings which avarice brings
    To crush out our existence.

Now, woman, we will stand by thee
    In fair and adverse weather;
Come, thou, help us with votes, and thus
    We all shall pull together.

With one voice ask, and then the task
    Of equal rights securing—
Long since begun—at once is done;
    And done to be enduring.

With faith in right, we'll then have might
    To stem all adverse currents,
And reach a port of safe resort
    In spite of winds and torrents;

While those who ride upon the tide,
    When tidal waves are flowing,
And shift their range as tides may change,
    Or winds reverse their blowing,

Find winds that blow with tidal flow,
    Reversed, can but condemn them;
And ebbing waves must find them graves,
    Unless for right they stem them.

PIQUA, OHIO, March 1, 1874.

APPENDIX.

I.

FORMS OF PLEDGES.

The following are the forms of pledges used in the progress of the Woman's Temperance Movement:

DRUGGISTS' PLEDGE.

We, the undersigned, druggists of ———, hereby pledge ourselves, upon our honor as business men, that from this date we will, under no circumstances, sell, or give away, or allow to be sold or given away by any of our agents or employes, any alcoholic or intoxicating liquors, wine, beer, or ale, except upon satisfactory evidence that the liquors are to be used for medicinal or mechanical purposes.

PROPERTY HOLDERS' PLEDGE.

We, the undersigned, property holders in ———, pledge ourselves, upon our honor, not to let or lease our premises (or premises for which we are agents), in this city, or permit them to be used or occupied for the sale or dispensing in any way of spirituous liquors, wine, beer, or ale, to be used as a beverage.

DEALERS' PLEDGE.

We hereby pledge ourselves, upon our honor, not to sell, furnish, or give away, or allow to be sold or given away by any agent or employe of ours, either by retail or wholesale, any spirituous liquors, wine, beer, or ale, except for medicinal or mechanical purposes.

PHYSICIANS' PLEDGE.

We, the undersigned, physicians of ———, upon our honor as professional men, promise hereby not to prescribe the use of spirituous liquors, wine, beer, or ale, only in case of absolute necessity.

II.

CAMPAIGN SONGS.

New songs have not been received with much favor during this crusade, the ladies having as a rule preferred to sing the old familiar hymns, which everybody knows, and which are so admirably adapted to arousing the enthusiasm of devout Christians or workers in any great moral reformation. Such hymns as "Nearer my God to Thee," "All Hail the Power of Jesus' Name," "Praise God from Whom all Blessings Flow," "Rock of Ages," and the Battle Hymn of the Republic have arisen from every assemblage of the crusaders and have become as familiar to the saloon-keepers of Ohio as they have heretofore been to the most regular church-goers. To fit the air of the Battle Hymn of the Republic, or "John Brown," as it is generally called, several temperance songs have been written, and some of them have been sung by the ladies and mass meetings of both sexes, with great effect. We append three, which have been received with favor:

THE BATTLE HYMN OF TEMPERANCE.

BY LEWIS MEREDITH.

Tune: "*John Brown.*"

The word from Heaven is spoken, and will never pass away,
That truth and right shall spread, and win a universal sway;
And now are pouring o'er the world the glories of the day:
    God's truth is marching on.

CHORUS.

    Glory, glory, hallelujah!
    God's truth is marching on.

From sin and Satan Christ shall have the empire of the world;
Through darkest dens, o'er ranks of hell, His lightnings shall be
    hurled;
Behold from far, and waving wide, his banner is unfurled:
        His truth is marching on.

The wretched earth has mourned so long the reign of vice and
    crime,
That hearts will dance and eyes will shine when comes the better
    time.
'Tis coming! coming on apace! In all its golden prime:
        God's truth is marching on.

The fiend is doomed! THY will be done, by woman pledged and
    sworn.
The forts are stormed by prayer and praise, and on the wind is
    borne
Exulting shouts of joyful hosts, as through the gates of morn:
        God's truth comes marching on.

Arise with Heaven! and bless the world; let all respond below;
With heart and hand and voice arise, to fell and crush the foe;
For God hath cursed the curse of drink, and He will lay it low:
        His truth is marching on.
  CHICAGO, February 26, 1874.

BATTLE HYMN OF THE CRUSADERS.

" Mine eyes have seen the glory of the coming of the Lord,"
The fulfillment of His promise, as recorded in His Word,
And the smiting of the wicked with his "terrible swift sword."
        When God is marching on.

          CHORUS.
  Glory, glory, hallelujah! glory, glory, hallelujah!
  Glory, glory, hallelujah! our God is marching on!

Long hath God heard from stricken hearts a feeble, plaintive sigh—
"How long, O Lord, how long must we unpitied live and die?
Wilt Thou not in Thy mercy, Lord, now listen to our cry?
        As Thou art marching on?"

The woes of drunkenness on earth have mounted up to Heaven,
The wrongs of parents, children, wives, are known and unforgiven,
And long God's light and truth in vain with guilty men have striven;
    Now God is marching on.

In mighty power God's voice is heard above all earthly din,
Repent! repent! come forth at once from all your haunts of sin,
Ere in my courts I swear in wrath, "ye shall not enter in;"
    For God is marching on.

Long have you to your brother's lips a poisoned chalice pressed,
And though you know 'tis sin and crime, by you 'tis unconfessed;
Now listen to God's stern command this moment to desist,
    For God is marching on.

The sinner hears the voice of God now sounding in his ears,
It mingleth with kind woman's voice, in songs, and prayers, and tears,
And fills his heart with sense of guilt, and penitence, and fears;
    God's Truth is marching on.

He listens to the still small voice of conscience in his heart,
And pledges from iniquity forever to depart,
And in the cause of Temperance to take an earnest part;
    Our God is marching on.

Let all God's people lift their hearts, and from the mountain's top,
And from the plains and valleys deep, send up a joyful shout,
The Lord is God, and from the earth this curse he will blot out,
    For God is marching on.

THE BATTLE HYMN OF THE CRUSADE.

BY MRS. EMILY J. BUGBEE.

On the plains of bloodless battle, they are gathering true and strong,
All the hero-hearted women, who have wept in silence long,
At the terrible oncoming of this raven-winged wrong,
    Now God is leading on.

    CHORUS—Glory, glory, hallelujah, etc.

They have sallied forth to conquer, and will never beat retreat,
While the banner of the rum-fiend is still flaunted on the street,
And his hellish snares are waiting, for the all unwary feet,
   For God will lead them on.

They will pierce the bending heavens with united prayers and cries,
Till the strongholds shall be shaken and the foe defeated lies,
Who has slain his many thousands of the strong ones and the wise
   For God will lead them on.

They have looked to law's enforcement, for the time that never came,
Now, God hath surely kindled in their hearts undying flame,
And relying on His spirit, they shall conquer in His name,
   For He is leading on.

For the future of their dear ones, for their country's power and pride,
Onward moved by bitter memories of the past, whose pains abide,
They are working, weeping, praying, in their weakness side by side,
   For He is leading on.

Be still, oh tongue of caviler, be strong oh heart of fear,
See you not the cloudy pillar that is ever hovering near,
Know you not an ear is open that will not refuse to hear?
   For God is leading on.

Oh the beauty and the blessing when the curse is swept away,
That has turned to midnight darkness so many a golden day,
And is throwing weary shadows o'er many a life-long ray,
   For Christ is coming near.

All the desert and the wilderness shall blossom with the flowers
Of industry and plenty, in this blessed land of ours,
And the grace of God unstinted shall come down in gentle showers,
   For heaven will be begun.

III.

DIO LEWIS' ACCOUNT OF HIS MEETINGS IN WORCESTER—HIS PLANS FOR A NEW SERIES OF MEETINGS IN OHIO.

MONTPELIER, VT., March 9, 1874.

"*To the Editor of the Cincinnati Gazette:*

"The temperance meeting at Worcester was a grand success. The great hall was never filled with a nobler audience, and every one declared that the Ohio temperance movement was fairly inaugurated in the heart of Massachusetts. The meeting at Grace Church, the next morning—a meeting of women—filled the house; and was characterized by the same manifestations that have so constantly thrilled me in the Ohio meetings. I attended, likewise, the meeting of the clergy in the afternoon. It was long and inharmonious. The question was, whether, in the resolution which should express their views of the woman's temperance movement, they should say, '*Resolved,* That we shall *respect* any temperance movement inaugurated by our Christian women;' or, 'We bid *God speed* to any temperance movement,' etc. The meaning of 'respect' and 'God speed' were carefully considered. While this debate was in progress, there were six hundred tearful women on their knees in Grace Church.

"I have been lecturing in other localities every day since, but learn from the newspapers that the friends in Worcester have been very busy in devising what is to be known as the Eastern Woman's Temperance Movement. They propose to reduce the number of women in the parties visiting saloons, and to visit privately property owners, to induce them not to rent their property for dram selling; and, in case any property is already rented for this vile purpose, not to renew the lease. In every case they propose to avoid all excitement, which, it is affirmed, is inconsistent with the refined tastes of New England. I can not forsee the result. But one thing is very certain, the women of Worcester are desperately in earnest, and, I have no doubt, will find a way. I notice in Saturday's papers, in large letters,

"'DIO LEWIS' WESTERN SCHEME ABANDONED BY THE LADIES OF WORCESTER.'

"I am sure the brave women of Ohio will be glad to learn a better way, and will adopt the 'Eastern method,' or what a Boston paper calls the 'Worcester method,' if they can see in it some easier and more effectual way of ridding their great Commonwealth of the curse of dram shops.

"At the Columbus convention I gave notice that I should return to Ohio before the 15th of March. I must visit New York, Philadelphia, and some other cities, but think now I shall reach Cleveland on the evening of Monday, the 16th of the month. I particularly wish to begin in the northern part of the State.

"In every city, town, or village, where the friends will manage their meetings in a certain way, I will make no charge for my services beyond the mere expenses. There are several towns in Ohio which have written me their willingness to pay a hundred dollars if I would come to them. I will visit all of those towns, and any others, without charge, if they will make the following preparations:

"1. Charge an admission fee of twenty-five or fifty cents, to raise a fund to carry on the work, but admit women free. By the fee you keep out idlers.

"2. Reserve one-half the house, and that immediately in front of the platform, for invited women. Print invitation cards, and carefully circulate them among the best women in town, with a statement on the card that the ticket gives the bearer a reserved seat. These tickets are to be distributed fairly among the various churches, not neglecting the Catholic Church, and among many excellent women outside the churches. Ushers will receive the holders of such tickets and seat them.

"3. Circulate complimentary invitation cards to clergymen, and such other persons as the friends would like to have sit on the platform.

"4. Have a good singer on the platform, who, in addition to a leading voice, shall keep time with his hand, and thus help the whole audience to sing as with one voice.

"I will bring the songs. These will be distributed free through the house, to be preserved by the friends for use in future meetings.

"Although for the nineteen temperance meetings held in Ohio I received but $315, and after paying expenses from Boston throughout the campaign and back to Boston, including the expenses of some other people in part, and very large telegraph bills, I had less than $50 balance; and certainly it was the most exhaustive labor of my life, still I think now there was a sort of justice in the contemptuous sneer of the newspapers that 'Dio Lewis is praying for temperance at $50 a night.' I shall not expose myself to this criticism again. Few men sacrifice more than I do by absence from home, as I have two large institutions in which persons are occupied who are dependent on me for daily directions. But I am not a poor man, and am free to admit that it was wrong to charge a fee for conducting the temperance meetings. I will see that the balance left in my pocket goes back into the good work in Ohio.

"But let it not be forgotten that some most efficient and devoted laborers now at work in Ohio and other portions of the West are dependent upon their daily labor for their daily bread. Nothing would be more unjust and cruel than to ask these faithful friends to work for nothing."

THE WORK IN CINCINNATI.

At the time this volume goes to press the women of Cincinnati have entered, with much enthusiasm, upon the great work of redeeming that city. Prayer meetings of women, ministers, and business men, as well as great mass-meetings, attended by both sexes, are daily and nightly held. The Christian Women's Temperance League is officered as follows:

For President, Mrs. Charles Ferguson; First Vice-President, Mrs. W. H. Malone; Second, Mrs. M. B. Hagans; Third, Mrs. W. H. Allen; Treasurer, Mrs. Dr. E. Williams; First Secretary, Mrs. E. Dalton; Second Secretary, Mrs. E. S. Johnson.

The city has been divided into the following districts for the active work of visitation:

"Southeastern District—Boundaries: North Miami Canal; east, Mount Adams; south, Ohio river; west, Central avenue.

Subdivisions of the Southeastern District:

1—Court and Canal, Elm street, Eighth street Central avenue.
2—Eighth, Elm, Fifth, Central avenue.
3—Fifth, Elm, Pearl, Central avenue.

APPENDIX. 117

4—Pearl, Elm, river, Central avenue.
5—Canal, Vine, Eighth, Elm.
6—Eighth, Vine, Fifth, Elm.
7—Fifth, Vine, Pearl, Elm.
8—Pearl, Vine, river, Elm.
9—Canal, Main, Eighth, Vine.
10—Eighth, Main, Fifth, Vine.
11—Fifth, Main, Pearl, Vine.
12—Pearl, Main, river, Vine.
13—Canal, Broadway, Eighth, Main.
14—Eighth, Broadway, Fifth, Main.
15—Fifth, Broadway, Pearl, Main.
16—Pearl, Broadway, river, Main.
17—Eggleston avenue, Broadway, Fifth.
18—Fifth, Pike, Pearl, Broadway.
19—Pearl, Pike, river, Broadway.
20—Fifth, Eggleston avenue, river, Broadway.
21—Gilbert avenue, Mount Adams, Observatory street, Eggleston avenue.
22—Fifth and Observatory streets, reservoir, Ohio river, Eggleston avenue.

The remainder of the city was divided into districts, as are below described, and these districts are to be subdivided in the same manner as is above shown for the first district. The work of making this subdivision was committed to Dr. Walden, by whom the districting as above was also marked out on the map of the city:

2. Southwestern District—Boundaries: Hopkins street, Central avenue, Ohio limits, western limits.
3. Northwestern District—North of Hopkins street and west of Miami canal.
4. Northeastern District—North and east of the Miami canal.
5. Mt. Auburn District—Mt. Auburn and Corryville.
6. Walnut Hills District—Walnut Hills, Woodburn, East Walnut Hills, and west to limits of District No. 1.

7. Fulton District—Fulton, Pendleton, and Columbia.
8. Cumminsville District—Twenty-fifth Ward.

Friday, March 13th, was observed by the ladies of Cincinnati and Columbus as a day of fasting and prayer for the blessing of God upon the Women's Temperance Movement in those cities.

www.ingramcontent.com/pod-product-compliance
Lightning Source LLC
Chambersburg PA
CBHW031400160426
43196CB00007B/834